CAPE YORK
A 4·W·D EXPERIENCE

i

CAPE YORK
A 4·W·D EXPERIENCE

A TRAVELLERS GUIDE
BY LYNN & YVONNE FRASER

Published by Boolarong Publications

Front Cover: *Sunset over the Torres Strait*

Back Cover: *Traditional Island Dancer.*

Opposite Page: *This is your goal — The tip of Cape York*

First published in 1992 by Boolarong Publications
12 Brookes St., Bowen Hills, Brisbane Qld 4006.
Reprinted and Revised May 1993.
Reprinted and Revised March 1996.
Reprinted and Revised May 1998.

National Library of Australia
Cataloguing-in-Publication data

> Fraser, Lynn, 1949-
>   Cape York: a 4WD experience.
>
>   ISBN 0 86439 136 6.
>
>   1. Cape York Peninsula (Qld.) – Description and travel -
>   Guide-books. I. Fraser, Yvonne, 1950-   . II. Title.

919.43804

BOOLARONG PRESS
35 Hamilton Rd, Moorooka, Brisbane, Qld 4105.
Design and phototypesetting by Ocean Graphics Pty Ltd, Gold Coast, Qld.
Printed and bound by Watson Ferguson & Company, Brisbane.
Film Production by Sphere Color Graphics, Brisbane, Qld.

PROUDLY PRINTED
IN QUEENSLAND

CONTENTS

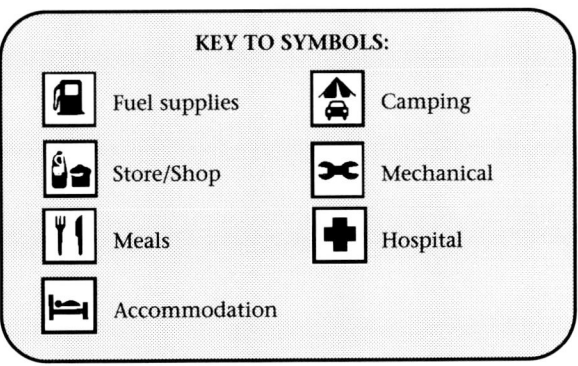

KEY TO SYMBOLS:

Fuel supplies

Camping

Store/Shop

Mechanical

Meals

Hospital

Accommodation

ACKNOWLEDGEMENTS

WE COULD not have compiled this book without the assistance of many people. We would sincerely like to thank the Queensland National Parks and Wildlife Service in Cairns and especially each individual ranger on the Cape for their valuable contributions. We would also like to thank Comalco for their information on Bauxite mining, and each station owner and business on the Cape for their assistance. Special thanks to the Royal Flying Doctor Service for their help and advice and the Royal Automobile Club of Queensland in Cairns and Brisbane for their assistance. To all the fellow travellers we met on our trips thank you, your comments and suggestions were invaluable in the preparation of this book. Last but not least our sincere gratitude to our secretary Carolyn Knell for her patience and dedication in the draft preparations.

REFERENCE BOOKS

In researching historical information for this book, many sources were used. Some information was derived from the publications below and we recommend their reading for more detailed accounts of Cape York's early history.

The Last Frontier	- Glenville Pike.
Queen of the North (A Pictorial History of Cooktown and Cape York Peninsula)	- Glenville Pike.
Cape York, The Savage Frontier	- Rodney Liddell.
Wings Across the Sea	- John J.E. Done.
The Torres Strait People and History	- John Singe.
The Holland Family Lockerbie, Cape York	- A.M. Hall.

The authors: Photographers Lynn and Yvonne Fraser

Opposite Page: Spectacular views of the Great Barrier Reef which fringes the Eastern Coast of Cape York

PREFACE

CAPE York Peninsula is all that area of Queensland lying North of a line drawn from just below Cairns on the East coast, across to Normanton on the South East corner of the Gulf of Carpentaria. This great triangle measures about five hundred kilometres across its base and tapers away Northward for about eight hundred kilometres until its final finger, Cape York, points to the sagging underbelly of New Guinea, just North across Torres Strait.

On the Eastern side of the Peninsula, from Cairns to Cooktown, rainforest clad mountains slope steeply down out of the clouds until their feet are washed by the jewelled Coral Sea. North of Cooktown the country is drier, alternating between Sandstone and Granite areas, timbered with open forests of Eucalypts. Near Princess Charlotte Bay the coast range again rears up high enough to attract sufficient rain for a jungle of vegetation which extends North to the Pascoe River, then gives way to a low scrub of Eucalypt and Teatree which covers the upper Peninsula.

Along the entire Peninsula the East coast ranges slope away Westward until they vanish in an undulating sea of grey-green Eucalypts. Rivers which rise in these ranges meander Westward through the forest, their waters mostly hidden under wide sandy beds until they emerge amongst mangroves to join the grey waters of the Gulf of Carpentaria.

Apart from the coastal ranges, the other main geographic features are a narrow belt of Limestone outcrops, once an ancient coral reef, which extends from Chilligoe to North of the Palmer River and the sandstone plateau that extends in a wide belt South West from Cooktown for over 200 kilometres to the Palmer River.

There are only two seasons in Cape York Peninsula, the "wet" and the "dry". The wet is easily the most spectacular, usually heralded in November by mighty thunderstorms, then becomes earnest at the end of January when the Inter-tropic Front sags Southwards and engulfs the Peninsula in a mass of humid air. By the end of March or early April the wet has spent its strength and retreats Northward, pursued by the bustling South East trade winds which proceed to dry out the sodden land and restore normality to nature.

PERCY TREZISE
Author/Artist

A Note From The Authors: We are now based on the Atherton Tablelands where we have opened a Outback Tourist Information Centre and Coffee Shop. You can call in en-route to Cape York and we will be able to supply up to date road information on the Cape and any other additional information you require, and we are only too happy to sign your book. **"The Down The Track Cafe And Outback Tourist Information Centre"** is located on the Millaa Millaa – Malanda Road at Tarzali, Atherton Tablelands, Qld. Drop in and see us.

Lynn & Yvonne Fraser.

INTRODUCTION

CAPE York is a large area of undeveloped land. It is a wilderness area of incredible contrasts. Dusty tracks, abundant river systems, crystal-clear creeks and spectacular waterfalls. There are breathtaking beaches, rich rainforest areas supporting varied flora and fauna. From the wild untamed bush to the friendliness of the people of the Torres Strait, Cape York will surprise and delight any visitor.

If you are looking for a holiday with a difference, then Cape York is for you. It is accessible to all people from all walks of life and of all ages. With new and upgraded roads throughout the Cape, more extensive fuel outlets and expanding facilities, it is now easier to travel to Australia's most Northerly mainland point, making Cape York an ideal location to get away from the pressures of everyday life.

In this book we have provided basic, practical information to assist visitors driving themselves to this area. We have also included examples of other ways to explore the Cape York region. Whether you drive yourself, choose a tour operator, fly, or ride a motorcycle, Cape York offers an adventure of a lifetime.

This publication is now in its fifth year and we are pleased with the feedback we have received from visitors to this area on the accuracy of this book. This was recognised at the 1994 Queensland Tourist Awards where we received an award as finalist in the Media Print Section for the research and accuracy of "Cape York A 4WD Experience". Cape York is undergoing a lot of changes and we will continue as we have in the past to keep the travelling public up to date through regular amendments to this guide.

When travelling the Cape, in order to preserve this delicate area, we ask that you take all rubbish with you if no disposal point is nearby and extinguish all campfires before leaving. Please respect the environment so future generations will be able to enjoy this unique part of Australia. Much of the area is now covered by Aboriginal lands and National Parks and you are asked to respect community laws and National Park regulations. We have outlined in this book where permits are required and where to contact the relevant authority. Access across private property is also now restricted, so please respect landowners' privacy.

At this time Cape York is untouched, providing a valuable insight into this unique land mass steeped in beauty and history. Any visitor to this area can successfully and safely complete the trip to the top with sensible planning. If you are in a hurry then Cape York is not for you. To fully appreciate the wilderness value of this area you need to take your time. Through this book we have included information which we hope will answer most questions and assist you in planning your trip to Cape York. We hope you enjoy Cape York as much as we do, and please take only photographs and leave only footprints.

Overleaf: Cape York — Please take only photographs and leave only footprints

"DIP" — You better believe it

Cape York's roads are continually changing each year with the wet season causing erosion washouts and the flushing out of large quantities of loose sand along many of the roads and tracks. The only advice that we can offer to the traveller is to be extremely aware at all times to sudden road changes.

There is very little signage located on the Cape's roads, so keep check on your kilometres travelled from intersections, roadhouses or any other major landmarks located on our maps. However, there is one sign located in numerous locations along the road, "DIP", and you better believe it. Slow down at all dip signs because at the bottom of some of these dips there can be a large washed-out section of roadway ready to wreak havoc on your vehicle.

The road's conditions can change from narrow loose sand to a well-formed and compacted surface then back to sections of bulldust all within a matter of metres, but you can be assured that whatever section of road you travel on will be corrugated.

Access to fuel supplies is tending to become less of a problem throughout the Cape. On the main road, 390km is the longest stretch between refuelling points at Archer River Roadhouse to Bamaga, with fuel also being available at Seisia. As to fuel usage, only you and your vehicle can judge the distance between refuelling stops, but be warned that the soft corrugated roads mixed with slow going can cause fuel consumption to skyrocket.

If you have to carry jerrycans for fuel, for most of the time these can be left empty, only filling them before entry to the most remote areas of the Cape. **LPG FOR CARS NORTH OF COOKTOWN IS TOTALLY UNAVAILABLE. THE BEST TIME TO TRAVEL TO THE CAPE IS BETWEEN MAY AND NOVEMBER. DURING THE WET SEASON THE ROADS ARE IMPASSABLE.**

Before embarking on your trip call the RACQ on 07 4033-6711 for the Road Conditions Report (24 hours service).

Weather Conditions

During the dry season the temperatures on the Cape vary only approximately 10°C from a yearly average high of 31°C to a yearly average low of 21°C. Slightly lower temperatures can be found on the Eastern coast in the more mountainous regions around the Cooktown and Iron Range areas.

Rainfall throughout the Cape York Region during the dry season is minimal with Weipa's average approximately 9mm per month increasing marginally along the East coast again around the Iron Range area.

Along the Eastern coast of Cape York and across the tip the notorious South East winds blow for days at a time making camping quite intolerable at times.

What to Take With You

As the temperature on the Cape between May and November is between 21°C - 31°C you only need to take lightweight clothes, plus a sweater or tracksuit for any cool nights. Include joggers or sandshoes and a hat and sunscreen for protection from the sun.

The Silent Sentinels of Cape York

A typical Bush Camp on the Wenlock River bed

Camping

Tents, table and chairs should be as lightweight as possible, a tarpaulin as protection from the sun is also recommended. As a lot of the camping is bush style a bar-b-cue plate and a grill stand is also recommended, billies are ideal for heating water and cooking food. You will need an esky to keep food cold, although we found the 3 way refrigerator the best as ice can become scarce away from the main centres. For storage of supplies the large plastic containers with sealable lids are ideal as they minimise the dust getting in. An easy way to do the washing is whilst you are travelling. A bucket with a water-tight lid serves as a washing machine. Half fill the bucket with water, add detergent and clothes and let the corrugations do the rest.

Care for the Environment

One of the biggest problems facing travellers to the Cape is the matter of rubbish disposal. There is a very simple solution to this problem. BURN ALL RUBBISH in the campfire, rake from the coals all unburnt rubbish, this in turn is crushed and placed in a plastic garbage bag and taken with you to rubbish disposal points referred to throughout this book. Disposal of rubbish this way decreases its volume and sterilises it leaving no odours. You had room in your vehicle to bring it in you have room to take it out with you.

Vehicle Preparation

In the research and photography for this book we travelled extensively throughout the Cape. Before departure our 4WD was fully serviced and inspected, everything was in first class condition. During our 4,500km trip around the Cape little mechanical problems began to show up like the spot welds on the fan shroud began to fracture, sump guards cracked and became loose, U bolts became loose all due to millions of road corrugations. Limping back into Cairns with a wired up fan shroud, virtually no top rubber bushes in the shock absorbers and a rebuilt engine mount (that had been skilfully repaired by Kjell at Seisia Marine Engineering), we wondered how people could possibly cope if they never have there vehicle thoroughly checked over by a reputable 4WD mechanic.

Before embarking on your Cape York trip make sure your 4WD vehicle is in top mechanical condition and fully serviced prior to your departure. Most importantly pay particular attention to your suspension system as these components take the brunt of all 20 million plus corrugations so all pins, bushes, "U bolts" and springs, shock absorbers and all rubber mountings should be checked by a competent mechanic.

Tyre Services 4WD — Cairns

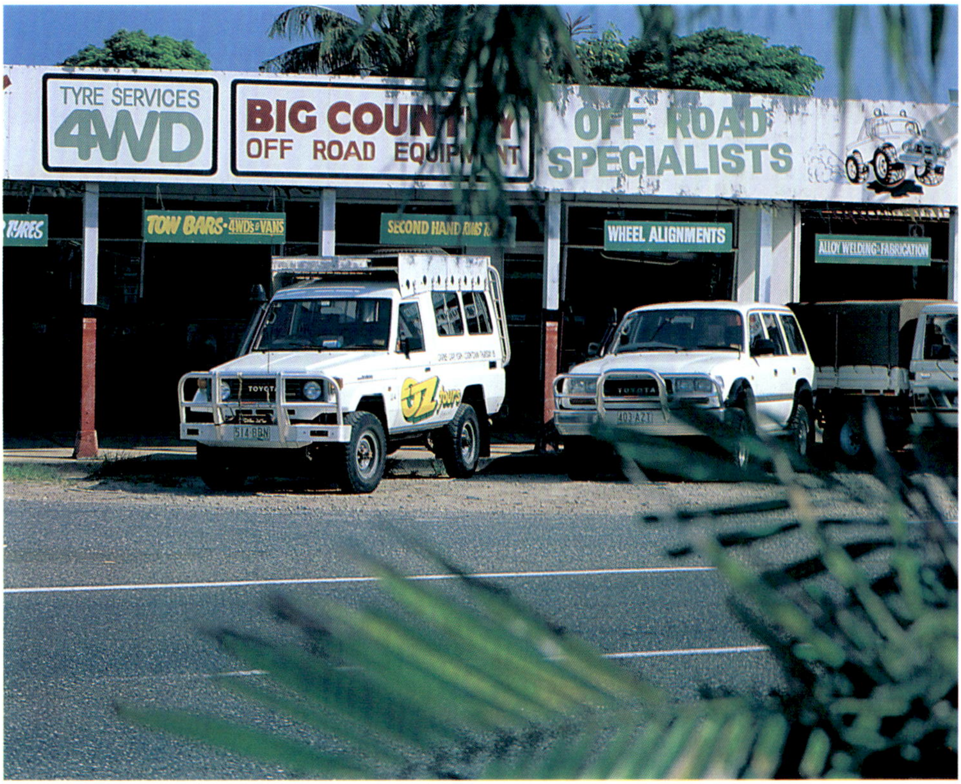

TYRE SERVICES 4WD are located in Cairns and Townsville and know the rigours of Cape York travel and have tailored their 4WD business to the preparation and servicing of vehicles to meet the needs of the Cape's roads. As the Cape's roads are unlike any other road in Australia, Tyre Services 4WD know exactly what to look for in vehicle preparation, from the choice of tyres to suspension and steering right down to a recommended minimum list of spare parts and safety equipment required for your trip.

TYRE SERVICES 4WD offer an impressive list of 4WD services, repairs, after market products and a hire service for winches, tree guards, high-lift jacks and roof racks to make your trip to the top a safe and trouble-free one.

Care for the environment when winching.
Please use a tree guard

Coopers Tires are America's most trusted 4WD tyre with up to 80,000 kms guarantee in writing on most popular sizes. How can a tyre company boast of such a guarantee? Coopers Tires have been manufacturing tyres since 1914, advancing through the years utilising the best of all the world's new technologies, but never losing sight of lessons learnt in the past. Coopers Tires are still made heavier and stronger than most other tyre manufacturers' products, thus giving you the edge in traction and mileage guarantee in writing. For a full list of Coopers Tires distributors contact:
Exclusive Tyre Distributors, 975 Ipswich Road, Moorooka, Qld. 4105.
Phone: (07) 3892-2533. Toll Free 1800 681 298.

TYRE SERVICES 4WD recommends the use of a quality tyre such as Coopers Tires, and they must be in good condition before you depart. Do not be fooled into using old three-quarter worn-out tyres with the intention that they will get totally hacked about on the Cape roads and then when you get home fit your 4WD with a new set as a reward for a trip well done. This is false ecomony, as you most probably will find that halfway through your trip you could be up for a new set of tyres due to tyre fatigue, staking or side-wall damage.

When you are having your tyres checked or changed and you are not quite sure how to go about repairing a puncture, tell the technician where you are headed and ask if he can give you some instructions so you can repair your own punctures if necessary on the road. If you have been travelling through loose and boggy sand and have deflated your tyres, pump them up again as soon as you reach a firm, solid base. Always run your tyres at the manufacturer's recommended pressure. Don't be lulled into the practice of running under-inflated tyres to smoothe out road corrugations as this is one sure way to tyre damage, let alone a very dangerous driving practice.

TYRE SERVICES 4WD Recommends

The best advice we can give you when travelling on Cape York is to keep your load as light as possible. Leave behind the T.V.'s, hairdryers and electrical appliances. Take only the essential items that you will use in a bush camping situation. Most suspension damage occurs due to overloading your vehicle, so please travel as light as possible.

TYRE SERVICES 4WD Recommends

As the temperature on the Cape can range up to the mid 30°C your engine's cooling system should be in top condition. The radiator should be cleaned inside and out and the whole cooling system pressure tested for leaks, and any soft, cracked or damaged heater or radiator hoses should be replaced before departure.

CAUTION: Never remove a radiator cap from an over-heated engine until it has had sufficient time to cool.

TYRE SERVICES 4WD Recommended spares and repair equipment:

Hand-operated winch (unless your vehicle is already fitted with a winch).
Two metal jerrycans for fuel.
Water container (enough water for a total cooling system refill).
Tool kit suited to your vehicle.
Puncture repair kit.
Tyre levers.
Tyre pump and pressure gauge.
One spare tyre casing.
Two spare inner tubes and valves.
Spare fan and air-conditioner belts.
Spare fuel and oil filters.
A selection of nuts, bolts and screws to suit your vehicle.
Quality tested jack.
Tow rope (proper snatchem type).
Torch.
Axe.
Shovel.
Full selection of lubricants, engine, transmission, power steering oils.
Brake and clutch fluids, grease and dewatering fluid for electricals.
Tree guard (for winching).
10m soft 10g tie wire (very important).
2 rolls cloth bound gaffa tape.
1 roll electrician's tape.
Selection of fuses.
Jumper leads (good quality).
Top and bottom radiator hoses.
The above list of items are classed as essential items, and you should not leave on your trip until you have them all.

For further information contact:

Tyre Services 4WD Cairns
247 Mulgrave Road
Cairns 4870. Qld.
Ph: 0740 51-9375 Or 0740-51-9122
Fax: 0740 34-1569

Tyre Services 4WD Townsville
Cnr. Bayswater Rd. & Duckworth St.
Garbutt 4814. Qld.
Ph: 0747 79-4299
Fax: 0747 25-1308

Leave your garden trailers at home

Roof Racks

If you intend using a roof rack make sure you use a very strong and sturdy one with several strong roof attachment points. Remember when using a roof rack you are altering your vehicle's centre of gravity (making it top heavy) and therefore making your vehicle less stable and easier to roll over when negotiating creek crossings or undulating country.

Instead of buying a roof rack give serious consideration to a rear bumper tyre carrier. These type of carriers can carry jerrycans for fuel and water plus your spare tyre, giving a much lower centre of gravity and thus a much higher margin of safety. If you have to use a roof rack remember to pack all your heavier items as low as possible on the floor of your vehicle working upwards to the lightest on the roof rack.

Trailers

The only trailers to use on the Cape roads are the specially built off-road type with 16" wheels, very strong axles, springs and tow couplings. The only thing we have to say about your 6" x 4" garden-type trailer, boat trailers and camper-type trailers are to "leave the damn things at home or in storage in Cairns". Joes Airport Lockup and Storage can take a load off your vehicle with storage facilities for all your extraneous trailers, campers and luggage.

Joes Airport Storage, 116 Anderson St, Cairns. Qld. 4870. Ph: 0740 53-1647.

Suspensions

The true test of a good suspension system is in its off-road performance. Wilkinsons' of Atherton have been manufacturing springs and suspensions for many years and have proved their reliability on Australia's toughest test track, the road to Cape York.

The authors and Australia's largest off-road tour operator, Oz Tours, exclusively use and recommend Wilkinsons' suspensions because of their ability to be vehicle matched and load rated to suit your individual specifications.

For all information regarding your suspension system contact:

Wilkinsons', 1 Gill Street, Atherton, Qld. 4883. Ph 0740 91-1328
Fax 0740 91-1653. For after hours service. Ph: 0740 91-2434.
or **Tyre Services 4WD – Cairns.**

Automobile Clubs

There are a number of benefits to being a member of an Automobile Club, especially the extra services offered when travelling. With reciprocal rights throughout Australia club membership is worthwhile in the case of a breakdown and towing services over and above the normal membership conditions, giving greater security if you breakdown in a remote area. Some examples of the help you can obtain with the PLUS membership are:

1. 3 nights accommodation and Car Hire whilst awaiting vehicle repairs.
2. 5 days Car Hire (no accommodation)
3. Transportation of passengers and vehicle to your home destination for repairs in the case of serious damage to your car
4. Leave the vehicle for repairs, passengers are transported home (with a return trip for one to collect repaired vehicle).

On arrival in Cairns before you embark on your trip to Cape York contact the RACQ in Sheridan Street, Cairns to obtain an up to date report on the conditions of the roads in this area or phone the 24-hour service Road Conditions Report on: 0740 33-6711.

For information on membership and extra services contact your Automobile Club in your state.

AUTOMOBILE CLUBS
ROYAL AUTOMOBILE CLUB OF VICTORIA (RACV)
550 Princes Highway
Noble Park 3174
VICTORIA
Ph: 131 955.
NATIONAL ROADS & MOTORIST'S ASSOCIATION (NRMA)
151 Clarence St
SYDNEY 2000
Ph: 132 132.
ROYAL AUTOMOBILE ASSOCIATION OF SOUTH AUSTRALIA INC (RAASA)
41 Hindmarsh Square
ADELAIDE 5000.
Ph: (08) 8202 4600.
THE ROYAL AUTOMOBILE CLUB OF W.A. (RACWA)
228 Adelaide Tce
PERTH 6000
Ph: (08) 9421 4400.
THE ROYAL AUTOMOBILE CLUB OF TASMANIA (RACT)
Cnr Patrick & Murray Streets
HOBART 7000
Ph: (03) 6232 6300.
AUTOMOBILE ASSOCIATION OF NORTHERN TERRITORY (AANT)
79 - 81 Smith Street
DARWIN 0800
Ph: (08) 8981 3837.
THE ROYAL AUTOMOBILE CLUB OF QUEENSLAND (RACQ)
520 Mulgrave Road,
Earlville. Cairns 4870.
Ph: 131 905.
300 St. Pauls Terrace Fortitude Valley BRISBANE 4005 Ph: 131 905.

Financial Facilities on Cape York

Banking facilities are limited in the Cape York area. There are a few Commonwealth and National Bank outlets as listed throughout this book and one Westpac located in Cooktown. However, most outlets now have EFTPOS, enabling the traveller to access cash more easily. Travellers Cheques are still another option, and the majority of outlets we spoke to are happy to cash or exchange them for goods. The advantage of Travellers Cheques is the security of replacement should they be lost or stolen. A phone card is also handy.

Ampol Card

Another valuable asset when travelling Australia is the Ampol Card. Running low on cash is a constant worry, but being an Ampol Card holder you will never be faced with this problem. You can use the Ampol Card at most Ampol Service Stations in Australia to purchase fuel, oil, batteries, tyres, in fact anything you require including all sundry items. Each month you receive a printed statement of purchases made, enabling you to make one easy, interest-free payment. Outlets on Cape York accepting the Ampol Card are listed throughout the book. Application for this card can be made at your nearest Ampol Service Station.

FRUIT FLY QUARANTINE AREA – In order to stop the spread of this pest on Cape York checkpoints have been set up by the Department of Primary Industries at Laura for north-bound travellers and now at Coen when heading south on certain items. A long list of fruits and some vegetables are prohibited past this point unless purchased from a approved outlet complete with a certificate which must be presented at the checkpoint. You must stop and have your vehicles inspected. In order to know exactly what you can carry with you and where to purchase certified fruit and vegetables, contact the DPI.

The DPI has announced the fruit-fly problem is diminishing, so it is possible some checkpoints may have ceased operation. Phone the DPI on FREE CALL 1800 650 268 for the latest information *before embarking on your trip.*

Royal Flying Doctor Service of Australia

The Royal Flying Doctor Service (RFDS) plays a vital role in providing a comprehensive medical service to people in remote areas of Australia.

It became operational on May 15th 1928. Its founder was the very Rev John Flynn, a missionary who originally began his work in 1912 when only 2 doctors served an area of some 300,000 square km in Western Australia and 1,500,000 sq km in the Northern Territory. It did not take him long to realise that air transport and radio were needed to break the isolation of the inland and to provide adequate medical care for its people. Aircraft at that time were not suited for ambulance work and radio then was still in its infancy, so it was many years before his vision of a Flying Doctor Service became a reality, but John Flynn worked towards his goal and the birth of the Service in 1928. It was known then as the Aerial Medical Service and was under the contract of the Australian Inland Mission. The first flying doctor was Dr. K. St. Vincent Welch and the first flying doctor pilot was Arthur Affleck of Qantas. Qantas under contract to the missions provided the pilot, aircraft and servicing, and in those days was a small bush airline known as Queensland and Northern Territory Aerial Services (Q.A.N.T.A.S). Today it is a major international airline.

The first aircraft to be used by the RFDS was a De Havilland DH-50A, a single-engined timber and fabric bi-plane. The service's first base was at Cloncurry, Western Queensland, but there was no radio communication between the base and outstations. What was needed was a cheap and reliable two-way radio. This was a tall order in those days due to radio's infancy, but a young Australian radio engineer, Alfred Traeger, solved the problem. He developed a two-way radio set which he thought would be suitable for the outstations. After overcoming many problems the famous pedal wireless was created, where the operator powered the generator by pedals, just like riding a bike. At first messages were sent in Morse code. Later came the development of a keyboard transmitter, and finally speech and voice transmission. Sets later were powered by car batteries, replacing the pedals.

The pilots in those early days had to operate sometimes under very difficult conditions. Airstrips often left much to be desired and there was the lack of navigational facilities and airstrip lighting. Many of the areas they had to fly into were not mapped and if they were, the maps were unreliable, so pilots had to know their landmarks. As aviation advanced, navigational aids improved and aircraft became fully instrumented, allowing all weather and night flying, but even today there are some remote areas where navigational aids are not available and pilots must still fly visually by dead reckoning.

In the 1930's the Australian Inland Mission relinquished its contract over the service and a national organisation was formed with sections in various States. It was renamed the Australian Aerial Medical Service. It changed its name again in 1941 to become the Flying Doctor Service. The prefix Royal was granted by the Queen in 1955. Throughout the 1930's other sections were formed in N.S.W., Vic, Western Australia, South Australia and Northern Territory. Today the RFDS operates from bases throughout Australia. Each base provides an emergency evacuation service to the sick and injured, giving immediate medical attention to the patient before being transported to a larger medical centre.

Regular clinical services are provided to each region on a rostered basis, and advice by telephone is given in hundreds of cases in which an illness is not serious enough to warrant a flight. To facilitate this, the Commonwealth

Government, through the RFDS, supplies standard medical chests which are kept at each homestead, mining camp etc, and the patient is instructed as to which medication to take by referring to a numbered list. The contents of the medical chests are provided free by the Commonwealth Department of Health.

When travelling in the Cape York region you are under the "mantle of safety" of the RFDS base in Cairns should you have a medical emergency, and the base can by contacted by telephone or radio. Most homesteads and facilities, police and rangers have STD telephones and radios, but there are a number of public telephones situated throughout the Cape. Before embarking on your trip we suggest a visit to the RFDS base in Cairns. The staff there will assist you with any enquiries regarding medical assistance if you have an emergency on the Cape. If you have a licensed radio, you can register your call sign at the base. If you are unsure of how to use your radio in case of an emergency you are urged to obtain a user's guide, which is free of charge. It outlines all the procedures for contacting RFDS. Also at the base is a visitors centre. During your visit you can experience a day in the life of the Flying Doctor, by watching a video. There's a demonstration of Traeger's pedal radio, with a display of original medical equipment, plus an extensive photographic display which takes you back to the early 1900's. The service relies on donations and public support. There is a wide range of gifts and mementos at the centre, and anything you purchase contributes to continuing this service. There is also a small entry fee into the centre, which is part of raising funds.

Medical Hints

Because the Cape is a remote area you will need to be self-sufficient. There are a few precautionary measures you should take. You should be in reasonable health; if a particular ailment is troublesome see your local doctor before you leave; if a tooth is giving you trouble see your dentist. If you require any special medication make sure you have an ample supply before leaving home. Be familiar with first-aid procedures. It's recommended you take a St. Johns Ambulance First Aid Course so you understand mouth-to-mouth resuscitation, haemorrhage control etc. Carry a St. Johns First Aid Manual in your vehicle. It is also recommended you buy a first aid kit. St. Johns have a good range of first-aid kits to suit all needs. Your local branch will be happy to supply information and advice on request. In particular make sure you carry vinegar for marine stingers and a bandage for snake bite and familiarise yourself with the first aid for both before you leave (by reading your first-aid manual or doing a first-aid course). If you plan to be isolated for a long time you may need a Royal Flying Doctor Service medicine chest rather than a first-aid kit (phone the nearest RFDS Base to where you are going for advice).

The Royal Flying Doctor Base and Visitors Centre can be located at:
1 Junction Street,
Edgehill Cairns 4870

Visitors Centre:
Ph: 0740 53-5687
Fax: 0740 32-1776
Base: 0740 53-1952 Business hours.

To contact the RFDS by telephone –
All medical enquiries Ph: 0740 53-5419
(24 hrs)

Medical and Hospital Facilities
Cooktown	-	0740 69-5433
Coen	-	0740 60-1141
Weipa	-	0740 69-9155
Lockhart River	-	0740 60-7155
Bamaga	-	0740 69-3166
Thursday Island	-	0740 69-1109

Police Stations
Cooktown	-	0740 69-5320
Coen	-	0740 60-1150
Weipa	-	0740 69-9119
Lockhart River	-	0740 60-7120
Bamaga	-	0740 69-3156
Thursday Island	-	0740 69-1520

All police stations on the Cape are equipped to call the Royal Flying Doctor Service. Only call them for assistance in an emergency.

LIVING WITH THE WILDLIFE

Crocodiles

There are two species of crocodiles inhabiting the Cape York Region. The freshwater crocodile is only found in freshwater streams and lakes. They can bite if threatened and should be left alone.

The Estuarine (Saltwater Crocodile) is the one to watch out for. These animals are extremely dangerous and inhabit all rivers and creeks throughout the Cape and its coastal regions, making swimming extremely dangerous. We must accept crocodiles as part of our environment, so being aware and cautious will minimise the risks to humans. Some simple precautions are:

- Always pitch your camp at least 50m from the water's edge.
- Collect water using a bucket with a rope attached.
- If you must bath and wash up, choose a shallow spot, collect water and move away.
- Avoid swimming in areas where Estuarine Crocodiles are present.
- Avoid deep water pools and murky water.
- Do not prepare food at the water's edge.
- Canoeing and rafting is not recommended.

The Estuarine Crocodile is a protected species and should not be harmed in any way.

The Estuarine Crocodile

Snakes

Venomous snakes can be found throughout the Cape, including the Taipan, King Brown and Death Adder. Avoid walking through long grass and be particulary careful at creek banks and waterholes and wear good protective footwear. Know your first aid for snake bite.

Marine Stingers

Although the active stinger season is usually in the summer months, marine stingers can be found throughout the year on Cape York, the most dangerous being the Box Jelly. The safest way to avoid being stung is not to swim in the sea at all, again know your first aid treatment.

Bites and Stings

Mosquitoes and sand flies can be pests, so carry repellent. Wasps are very common, if you bump their nest they will swarm and attack, as the authoress found out after such an encounter receiving 64 very painful stings. A bite or sting cream will help, be cautious of these nests.

Fishing

If intending to do a spot of fishing on your trip give serious consideration about carrying a boat up to Cape York. The extra bulky weight of a boat and outboard plus all safety gear and fuel puts more strain on your 4WD's already stressed suspension, increasing your vehicle's fuel consumption, and also adding to a more stressed trip for the driver.

Save dollars and stress by leaving your boat at home or in storage at Cairns and consider using one of the professional fishing tours located throughout the Cape York region. These professional fishing operators know the area well and know the tides, moon phases, bait and what fish are running at the time you are visiting. So save money and many hours of tense driving carrying your boat up the Cape. Try the local fishing tours and really get amongst the Big Ones.

Fishing trips are located at Weipa on the West coast, and Seisia at the Top. Both locations offer excellent reef or estuary-type fishing, depending on your choice. Seisia Camping Ground has a small fleet of aluminium dinghies which you can hire for either half or full day's fishing.

If you are definitely a fishing person and intend taking your boat to Cape York please call into the Great Barrier Reef Marine Park Authority in Cairns – 10-12 McLeod St. Cairns 4870. Ph: 0740 52-3096 – and obtain the latest maps and regulations as to fishing the Cape. All of the Cape's East coast has many different marine zone types from line fishing only right through to areas of total preservation. Fishing in all National Parks is totally prohibited with heavy fines and confiscation of fishing equipment a very distinct possibility. Lakefield National Park is the only park which does allow a limited amount of fishing of its waterways. However, at the moment of writing this may all change as Lakefield National Park is under research as to it becoming a fish-breeding habitat with a total ban on all fishing within the park. Please call into one of the Rangers Stations located within the park and obtain the most up-to-date laws as to fishing within Lakefield National Park.

Fishing is excellent in the Cape York Region but you must observe legal lengths and return all undersized fish to the water, as this fisherman did with this Barramundi

Some Alternative Ways to Travel The Cape

There are many alternative ways to travel the Cape

OZ Tours Safaris know the Cape, and for those wishing to explore this area but having no desire to drive themselves or preparing their own meals, an Oz Tour is a wonderful alternative. Experience the lifestyle, the landscape and fauna & flora of the real Australia with the security and comfort of your Oz Tour guide and cook. Oz Tours Safaris are based in Cairns and are a family owned company. They operate 4WD tours to suit any need, and a wide range of wilderness holidays are offered that are suitable for all ages. You can choose between an outdoor camping safari or experience the pleasure of traditional Australian hospitality at motels, hotels, stations and lodge-style accommodation which can also be combined with a sea and air content. Whichever you choose you will experience the freedom and relaxation the Cape has to offer together with a friendly, personalised service. All tours are approved by the State Commissioner of Transport and Oz Tour Safaris are members of the Far North Queensland Tour Operators Association. All Oz Tours staff have extensive knowledge, and your guides are highly trained to give you an adventure of your lifetime. They operate a fleet of 16 4WD vehicles ranging from 7-24 seat capacity, including Landcruisers, Okas and Hinos.

Left: Top end fishing from the Seisia Jetty

HOLIDAY COMBINATIONS OFFERED
Camping Safaris

If you have limited time the 7-day 4WD overland/air safari is ideal. This safari will take you the entire length of Cape York Peninsula to Australia's most Northerly point and includes an optional cruise through the Torres Strait to visit Thursday Island. Combined with this is a spectacular scenic flight back to Cairns. Your flight is not designed to save time, but part of your holiday experience, giving you an overall view of this undeveloped land mass. Ten and 12-day tours are also available with a reverse itinerary.

For those with more time the 16-day overland safari gives the opportunity to explore the Cape York Region more extensively, including an optional visit to Thursday Island. Other highlights include Quinkan Aboriginal Painting, Cooktown, Weipa, Bamaga, the very top, Somerset and many other destinations.

An exclusive Oz Tours Package combines the tranquillity of a Coral Sea Cruise with a Cape York Overland camping safari. Combine the overland wilderness with a cruise through the tranquil waters of the Great Barrier Reef from Cairns to the Torres Strait. Definitely an exciting alternative. Twelve or 15-day tours are also offered.

Accommodated Tours

An 8-day 4WD accommodated wilderness tour offers an exciting overland expedition with the comfort of overnight accommodation combined with a scenic flight from Cairns to Bamaga. All accommodation in this sparsely populated area is utilised and you can enjoy Australian hospitality and cuisine in the outback tropics motels, hotels, stations and prestigious resorts. This tour also has a reverse itinerary. Another alternative is a 7, 10, 11 or 14-day overland safari combined with a leisurely Barrier Reef Cruise from Cairns to Torres Strait.

Tag-A-Long Guide Service

Tag-A-Long tours are designed for 4WD owners who want the thrill and satisfaction of exploring the Cape using their own vehicle with the security and backup of an experienced guide. Travelling in a convoy situation offers you independence with the highest degree of safety. For persons unfamiliar with off-road travel in wilderness areas this is an ideal service. Prior to departure full information is supplied on vehicle preparation, spares to carry, equipment required and advice on food supplies and how to store them. Your escort vehicle has full radio communication in the event of accident or breakdown. Your guide has mechanical and first-aid experience and will advise and assist you in all aspects of road conditions and creek and river crossings. A Tag-A-Long tour will completely make your holiday worry free, and any driver of average experience combined with commonsense and the willingness to follow advice will successfully drive to the Cape and back and enjoy every kilometre.

Experience a wilderness holiday with
OZ Tours Safaris

Additional Services Offered

For special interest groups, expert guides, academics and interpreters can be provided for fishing safaris, bird and wildlife spotting, Aboriginal art and culture, painting and photography. Whatever your requirement Oz Tours Safaris can tailor a tour to suit.

For further details on all tours contact:

Oz Tour Safaris,
P.O. Box 6464,
Cairns, Qld. 4871.
Ph: 0740 55-9535
Fax: 0740 55-9918

Exploring the Cape by Air

There is nothing so exciting as sitting back in the comfort of an aircraft to explore a remote area. For those who do not wish to endure corrugations and dust, this is an ideal alternative. Flightwest Airlines, Sunstate Airlines and Ansett Airlines all run scheduled flights to such areas as Weipa, Bamaga and Thursday Island. Below are some other options.

Wingz North Aviation have aircraft for charters, so you can explore all areas of Cape York and the Torres Strait. For all enquiries: Contact Wingz North Aviation, Hangar 9, General Aviation Section, Cairns Airport. Ph: 0740 35-9032.

The World's Longest Mail Run

Why not play Postie for a day and visit some of the world's most remote cattle stations? Cape York Air Services have a weekly mail run to Cape York, which provides a vital link to the outside world for residents of this remote area, especially in the wet season when the roads are closed. Residents rely on the mail plane not only for their mail in the wet, but also for fresh supplies. Cape York Air Services carries passengers both in the wet and dry seasons, and it is a fantastic way to see Cape York if you have very little time. Their aircraft are also available for charter. For full details contact: Cape York Air Services. Ph: 0740 35-9399. Fax: 0740 35-9108.

Left: Try a combination fly/drive holiday with Oz Tours Safaris.

Coach Services to Cape York

Coral Coaches operate a weekly service to Weipa. This service calls at all the main tourist facilities on Cape York Penisula en-route to Weipa. This allows you to plan your own trip if you do not have a 4WD or wish to go on an organised tour. Passengers can join the coach at either of the main pickup points at Cairns, Mareeba or Port Douglas, or at any other scheduled stop on Cape York Peninsula. They also operate a separate service to Cooktown.

For full details and schedules contact:

Coral Coaches
Ph: 0740 98-2600
Fax: 0740 98-1064

Experience breathtaking coastal views on your scenic flight

Cape York Motorcycle Adventures

For the motorcycle enthusiast, why not consider a Cape York Motorcycle Adventure? Based in Cairns, proprietor Roy Kunda, with 20 years' motorcycle experience, offers a two-wheel off-road adventure. Experience the thrill and freedom of riding to secluded areas, inaccessible even to 4-wheel drive vehicles, travelling along the old stock routes and trails of Cape York. One to 12-day safaris are available, with the choice of riding your own motorcycle or selecting from Roy's current Yamaha TTR range of hire bikes. Each safari has two guides with an extensive knowledge of the more remote areas of the Cape, and a 4WD support vehicle with a cook/driver. Meals, accommodation, camping equipment and fuel are all inclusive. When camping out you will enjoy Aussie-style bush tucker cooked over a camp fire. For groups of five or more a safari can be arranged to suit your personal needs. For motorcycle enthusiasts, an organised tour is recommended, as the support vehicle is equipped with a satellite phone and RFDS first-aid chest in the event of any emergency.

For further details contact:

Cape York Motorcycle Adventures
P.O. Box 105
Clifton Beach, Qld. 4879
Ph: 0740 59-0220 Fax: 0740 59-0801
Email: CYMCA @ IIG.COM.AU
Web Site: http://www.iig.com.au/cymca

*A Motorcycle Adventure through Cape York
is a must for all enthusiasts*

Vehicular Sea Ferries

If you are unfortunate enough to have a serious breakdown and have to transport your vehicle to Cairns, or wish to drive the Cape only one way, there are two barging services operating in this area. Seaswift visit Lockhart River and Bamaga and carry vehicles only. For information contact: Seaswift, 52 Tingira Street, Cairns, Qld. 4870. Ph: 0740 35-1234.

The Gulf Express carries vehicles and passengers. The fare includes all meals and shared cabin-style accommodation. The Gulf Express departs Cairns each Monday for Horn and Thursday Islands and departs for the return trip each Wednesday. For passengers who have driven up to Bamaga contact Horn Island on 0740 69-2009 to arrange the barging of your vehicle to Horn Island or Horn Island to Seisia. For full details contact: Jardine Shipping, P.O. Box 1867, Cairns, Qld. 4870. Ph: 0740 35-1299 or 0740 35-1900. Fax: 0740 34-1685.

Weipa to Karumba

Gulf Freight Services operate from Weipa to Karumba carrying both passengers and vehicles. For details contact: Gulf Freight Services, Yapa Street, Karumba, Qld. Ph: 0747 45-9333.

The Overland Telegraph Line

A few years after the discovery of gold in 1873 on the Palmer River, a telegraph line connected Cooktown to Brisbane with a branch line linking Old Laura to Palmerville.

In order to extend the electric telegraph line northwards the government sent John Bradford in 1883 to survey the Peninsula, his long and arduous trek north finally ended at Somerset. One year later the first section of the line was completed linking Fairview and Mein north of Coen, next the northern section of the line which ran through the country around the Jardine River was completed. A series of telegraph repeater stations were erected along the line and due to the hostility of Aboriginal tribesmen in the area, they were built like fortresses.

On the 23rd December 1886 Musgrave Station was opened and a few days later Coen. Mein was to follow in July 1887 with McDonnell and Patteson both opened on 25th August 1887. An underwater cable link to Thursday Island was also completed on 25th August 1887 allowing communication to Brisbane by morse code. The telegraph line opened in 1887 enabling the people of the Cape to overcome their loneliness, giving them a link with the outside world.

Maintaining the line was a never ending job, 2 or 3 men were employed at each telegraph station and for over 60 years they patrolled the line North and South on horseback. The last morse telegram to be sent from Brisbane to Thursday Island was on 24th June 1964, then messages were sent by a teleprinter radio channel, making the underwater cable obsolete.

The telegraph line remained in service until 1987 and was used as a local telephone line before being dismantled. Today nearly all properties and settlements on the Cape have an STD service through microwave towers scattered throughout the area. The telegraph track which it is now referred to still follows much of the original line north of Coen and is thoroughly recommended for its historic value when travelling.

There are many reminders on the Telegraph Track of bygone years

37

PAGE 39-73 OF THESE NOTES ARE TO BE READ IN CONJUNCTION WITH THE YELLOW ROAD ON THE REMOVABLE MAP AS THIS IS THE MOST SERVICEABLE ROAD TO THE TOP.

Cairns to Kuranda – 27km Bitumen

Climb up the Great Dividing Range through rainforest and over the Barron River.

Kuranda to Mareeba – 37km Bitumen

Leave the rainforests behind you and enter the farmlands where avocados, peaches and tobacco are grown. A visit to the Mareeba Heritage Centre at Centenary Park is a must. Ph: 0740 92-5674.

Mareeba to Mt Molloy – 40km Bitumen

From here to the Top the roads become unfenced so watch out for wandering stock.

Mt Molloy to Mt Carbine – 30km Bitumen

On the northern outskirts of Mt Molloy is a right-hand turn and this would lead you back to the coast and Mossman. Mt Carbine Roadhouse has fuel, meals and limited supplies, free camping and budget accommodation, plus mechanical assistance. Ph: 0740 94-3043. Opposite is the Mt Carbine Hotel/Motel. Ph: 0740 94-3108. The Mt Carbine Village & Caravan Park offers grassed, powered and unpowered sites, self-contained units, free caravan and trailer storage. For keen birdwatchers the bird life here is superb. Ph: 0740 94-3160.

Above: Cairns City the Gateway to Cape York

Left: Upgraded section of the Old Telegraph Track adjoining Bramwell Station

Spectacular views from Bob's Lookout

Mt Carbine to Palmer River – 84km Bitumen

26km out of Mt Carbine you will start to climb the Desailly Range to Bob's Lookout with its spectacular views. 8km past the Palmer River Roadhouse is the start of the dirt road, which extends all the way to the Top except for a few sections of bitumen through some of the towns.

Palmer River to Lakeland – 32km Dirt

16km past the Palmer River Roadhouse you start to descend down the Byerstown Range. Dust and large rocks make for slow going down this narrow section of road. Turn left for Cape York via Laura. Travelling straight through Lakeland is the road to Cooktown.

Lakeland is a small township located at the junction of the Cooktown and Peninsula Development Highways in the picturesque Laura River Valley and is the fastest growing and most productive farming area for its size on Cape York Peninsula. The area also boasts the largest coffee plantation in Australia, with over 130,000 mature trees.

Facilities in the township include a roadhouse with fuel, basic mechanical repairs, welding and limited grocery supplies. EFTPOS with all major credit cards accepted. Ph: 0740 60-2188.

The camping and caravan park close by offers powered sites and hot showers. Accommodation is also available at the Lakeland Downs Hotel/Motel. Ph: 0740 60-2142. All major credit cards accepted.

Lakeland to Laura – 60km Dirt

The road surface is quite hard with sections becoming corrugated. Closer to Laura the road is quite prone to dust holes. 47km from Lakeland on the left is Split Rock and Aboriginal paintings. This section of the road is bitumen.

Facilities at Laura

Laura is an old bush town with historical links to the Palmer River gold-rush era. There are a number of facilities offered here including the Quinkan Hotel and Camping Ground, with meals and takeaway food, accommodation and camping. Ph: 0740 60-3255. The Laura Cafe has fuel, meals and supplies. Ph: 0740 60-3230. EFTPOS facilities.

There's a caravan park opposite operated by the Ang-Gnarra Aboriginal Community. Ph: 0740 60-3214 for details.

The Lara Store and Post Office has fuel, ice, gas and groceries. Ph: 0740 60-3238. Accepted credit cards: Bankcard, Mastercard, Visa.

Contact the:
Aboriginal Rangers at the
Quinkan Reserve Information Centre on –
Ph: 0740 60-3214
for information about the Quinkan Rock Art and permits
to visit the art sites.
Laura Police Station
Ph: 0740 60-3244.

Old bush town of Laura

41

Quinkan Country

Quinkan Country extends some 6,000sq km of the South East Cape York Peninsula. Incorporated in this area is Lakefield National Park and Quinkan reserve, which extends from Laura to the coastline of Princess Charlotte Bay. This rugged terrain contains sandstone escarpments, open eucalypt woodlands and a network of river systems. Sandstone was layed down in the cretaceous era as the bed of a shallow coastal lake, weathering and erosion over 100 million years created today's "Sandstone Plateaux" and escarpments.

These provided rock shelters suitable for Aboriginal people to occupy during the wet season. Aboriginal people were living a traditional hunter-gathering way of life up until the Palmer River gold rush of the 1870's. The oldest known human occupation of rock shelters in the Quinkan area is dated to be 32,000 years.

The importance of this area was first recognised in 1959 by Captain Percy Trezise, an airline pilot, author/artist (now an acknowledged rock art authority) when he read a report of a road gang discovering Aboriginal paintings on a large slab near Laura.

After visiting the site he realised that this painting must be one of many located in the area, and began a program of exploration and recording of the Quinkan art. Following the discovery of the Split Rock gallery in 1959, some 1,500 sites have been recorded by Percy Trezise over the last 30 years on canvas. These canvases are now held in the archives of the Institute of Aboriginal Studies in Canberra. In order to protect the extensive body of rock art in the Laura district Percy Trezise strived to have the area declared a Reserve, this he achieved in 1975, ensuring the preservation of these ancient drawings for future generations.

Permission is needed from the Aboriginal Rangers at the Ang-Gnarra office to enter the Reserve and visit the sites. Other access is through the Trezise Bush Guide Service who are custodians of some art within their property. We thoroughly recommend a visit to this area as it provides a fascinating insight into these prehistoric sites and the Aboriginal way of life.

Trezise Bush Guide Service

Stephen Trezise began a bush guiding service specialising in the Quinkan rock art and wetlands of Lakefield National Park in 1980. Formerly a high school teacher he is now the proprietor of Jowalbinna Bush Camp and Deighton River Bush Camp and offers a bush guiding service to these fascinating areas.

Quinkan Country

43

Aboriginal Rock Art

Jowalbinna Bush Camp

This bush camp is situated in beautiful sandstone gorge country on the headwaters of the Little Laura River and offers comfortable accommodation, good food and showers and toilets. 1, 3 and 4-day safaris are offered and some of the highlights of your bush adventure include: the Aboriginal rock art of the Quinkan reserve, the wildlife and wetlands of Lakefield National Park and the historic ruins of the Palmer River gold rush. These interesting safaris provde great birdwatching and unique photographic opportunities and some real insights into the Australian bush and its fascinating human history. Trezise Bush Guide Service maximises the amount of time spent hiking these escarpments and pride themselves on really penetrating remote areas so visitors can experience the stillness and vastness of the Cape York Peninsula landscape.

Rock etching is the oldest form of rock art to be found in Australia

Deighton River Bush Camp

The Deighton River Bush Camp is situated in remote and rugged sandstone country. The Deighton River Valley has an ancient feel about it and the Aboriginal rock art here is spectacular. Sites visited include: Deighton Lady, Blue Figures, Rainbow Serpent and Rainmaking. You camp under canvas beside the river and each day hike into the hills.

Visitors driving themselves to the Laura district are welcome to visit Jowalbinna and Deighton River Bush Camps. 4WD is essential and maps are available from the Quinkan Hotel at Laura. As this area is privately owned there is no public access or camping. For all information on access to this area and tours offered

Contact:
Stephen Trezise
Trezise Bush Guide Service
P.O. Box 106,
Freshwater Cairns Qld 4870
Ph: 0740 55-1865

Laura to Hann River Roadhouse – 74km Dirt

2km out of Laura on your right is the Lakefield National Park turnoff. Straight ahead to Hann River. (Lakefield National Park detailed track notes page 141.) The road conditions vary from corrugations to sand-ridged vehicle tracks to bulldust holes. Slow down for the dips and creek crossings. The roadhouse is situated on the right, just North of the river.

Hann River Roadhouse

Situated next to the Hann River, the camping ground offers powered and unpowered sites with toilets, showers and laundry facilities. Meals are available at the licensed restaurant, there is fuel, a public telephone, limited supplies, bottled gas refills and EFTPOS facilities. Ph: 0740 60-3242.

Hann River to Musgrave – 62km Dirt

As the season progresses the road conditions deteriorate, so drive with caution on rough roads with dips and sandy sections. 18km further on is the right-hand run for Mary Valley Cattle Station and Wildlife Retreat. There is a camp ground, and accommodation consisting of two modern cabins and meals. Activities include bushwalks, tours and birdwatching. Ph: 0740 60-3254 for details.

Opposite the Musgrave Roadhouse is the turnoff to Lakefield National Park. 26kms along this road is Lotus Bird Lodge. This four star resort has cottage-style accommodation set alongside a lagoon and packages include all meals. There is a resident naturalist at the resort and activities include birdwatching and bush walking. There is also a swimming pool. For all enquiries contact: Lotus Bird Lodge. Ph: 0740 59-0773. Fax: 0740 59-0703. Freecall: 1800 674 974.

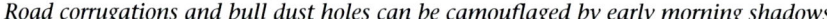

Road corrugations and bull dust holes can be camouflaged by early morning shadows

The original Musgrave Telegraph Station and Roadhouse

Musgrave

This historic fortress telegraph station was opened on 23rd December 1886 and was one of the many stations on the Cape providing a communications link. It closed as a telegraph station in 1928 and became a station homestead. Apart from the removal of the gun ports very few changes have occurred to the homestead and it has been preserved for its historical value.

Facilities

Musgrave now serves as a roadhouse. Fuel and limited supplies are available, spare parts can be obtained from Mareeba twice weekly and the mail plane operates a weekly service. There are also welding facilities here. The roadhouse is licensed and you can get meals and takeaway food, an STD telephone is located at the entrance, there is a public camping ground and some accommodation is available.

All major credit cards accepted. EFTPOS facilities.

Ph: 0740 60-3229.

Musgrave to Coen – 109km Dirt 🏠 🛒 🍴 🛏 ⛺ ✂ ✚

A right hand turn at Musgrave (due East of roadhouse) is the top road into Lakefield National Park (Lakefield National Park detailed track notes page 141) North of Musgrave you start to climb the Bamboo Range and this section of road can have a bad surface. North of the range the road traverses hilly country with some long and sudden dips, use caution.

About 27km from Coen you start on the new road, this section is quite good but don't overdo it speed wise as blow holes in the new road can catch you unaware. At the 27km mark South of Coen, turn right for Port Stewart and Silver Plains Station. (Port Stewart and Silver Plains detailed track notes page 139).

History of Coen

The discovery of gold in the 1870's in the Coen district first brought a flood of prospectors to the area, but this boom did not last long as the quantities of gold found proved to be a disappointment. Larger finds in other areas finally lured prospectors away and the gold fields of Coen were nearly all deserted. Despite the building of the Overland Telegraph Line in 1884 and the opening of the first school in 1885 and the Coen Telegraph Station two years later, the township remained a small and quiet settlement.

The discovery of large deposits of gold in 1893 by the Great Northern Mine really established the town and once again Coen was alive, 52,000ozs of gold was mined until its closure in 1916. The early 1920's saw further discoveries in the Batavia, Wenlock fields ensuring Coens survival. Through these years Coen became a centre for the people of outlying areas. They would come to town to collect their mail and supplies and recruit labour for their stations and mines.

For decades the Coen road was a pack horse track along the Overland Telegraph Line that ran from Laura to Bamaga, in 1928 the first car to travel to the top of the peninsula passed through Coen. Jim McDowell a pack horse mail man travelled this road regularly, he would start his run at Laura and deliver mail to stations en route before reaching Coen, this he did until 1951 when he died as a result of an accident involving his horse whilst on the track. He travelled the track for 13 years making him the longest serving pack horse mail man. Matt Gastelow then took over the run until Bush Pilots commenced deliveries of the mail by air later that year.

In 1943 Coen was flattened by a cyclone and had to be rebuilt. Alfred Colmen a carpenter, electrician and builder played a large part in the rebuilding of the township, by 1947 a new school had been built and the hotel and post office repaired.

Around 1950 the Telegraph Station was moved into Coen itself (today it is still standing and serves as a private residence). In 1958 Alfred Colmen helped to construct the Coen Children's Hostel and medical centre, enabling children from outlying areas to board at the hostel and attend school, as there was no church, a minister would visit the centre to conduct services. The hostel was also a focal point for social gatherings in those days and was popular as a community centre. Another school was built and opened in 1962 as the existing school was too small for the attending numbers. It was not until 30th November 1979 that Coen really stepped into the 20th century when it finally had a public electricity supply, followed by a direct dial telephone service and finally television in 1982 through a microwave link from Weipa.

The hostel closed down in 1985 and is now used as a medical centre, the Flying Doctors also hold their clinics there. Today Coen is a popular stop for visitors making their way to the top, enabling them to enjoy all facilities of modern day life.

Coen's Facilities

Situated right next to the Exchange Hotel on Regent Street is the service station, grocery store and mechanical workshop owned and operated by Peter and Gail Clark.

The grocery shop caters for all your needs. We suggest if travelling North that you stock your supplies here as Bamaga is the next major supermarket, quite a distance and higher prices may be experienced due to the remoteness.

The store has a large selection of fresh fruit and vegetables, frozen meats, bread and dairy products and a wide range of smallgoods, plus limited camping requirements and souvenirs.

The well-equipped workshop carries quite a range of parts, and if a part has to be ordered it can be obtained within 2 days. Fuel and oils, tyres and tubes are available and batteries are in stock. Compressed air is complimentary to all customers. If you are experiencing any mechanical problem, no matter how slight, we strongly suggest you have your vehicle checked here as there are no full mechanical services until Weipa – approximately 260km. If heading North, Bamaga is approximately 450km via the Bypass Road.

Other services offered include gas refills, ice and a fax machine is available for use. Trading is 7 days a week from 7.30am – 6.00pm but the workshop is not opened on Sundays. Accepted credit cards: Bankcard, Mastercard, Visa, Australian travellers cheques. Peter and Gail pride themselves on doing their best for a customer. They have a lot of knowledge, so if you need any assistance they will be only too happy to oblige. EFTPOS facilities.

Peter and Gail Clark
Regent Street, Coen
Ph: 0740 60-1144

Clark General Store and Garage, Main Street, Coen

Next to the Clark's General Store is the Exchange Hotel, commonly known as the "Sexchange Hotel" – besides a nice cold beer, motel-type accommodation is available, including single rooms, and meals are served. Ph: 0740 60-1133. Other accommodation in the town is at the Homestead Guest House on the other side of the Clark's store. You can choose between full accommodation or bed only. The guest house has 2 family rooms and 6 twin share. The complex is run by Mrs Irene Taylor – Ph: 0740 60-1157 for details and bookings. Across the road a camping ground is adjacent to the general store. Groceries and fuel are also available here – Ph: 0740 60-1134. There is also a cafe offering takeaway food and drinks, a post office with a Commonwealth Bank Agency and telephones. Emergency Nos: Police 0740 60-1150 Hospital 0740 60-1141.

If heading North this is the last main town for full supplies, banking etc. until Bamaga. There are a number of interesting locations in and around Coen that are worth exploring. At the back of the racecourse is the remains of the Great Northern Mine that once played such an important role in this area and is well worth a visit. 2km north of Coen is the Bend Camping Area on the Coen River. Camping is permitted along the river and there are toilets. This is also an ideal rest area and perfect for a picnic with plenty of sandy banks and shady trees.

The Ranger for Mungkan Kaanju National Park is located in Coen. The office is located at the old Telegraph Station Reserve on the northern edge of town. Turn left before the Coen River Bridge after crossing the Lankelly Creek (Irene Taylor Bridge). Here you can obtain information on the National Park and surrounding area. Because of the remoteness of Mungkan Kaanju you need to be totally self-sufficient. For full details: Ph: 0740 60-1137. Fax: 0740 60-1117.

Bend Camping Area – Coen River

Coen to Archer River Roadhouse – 66km Dirt ⛽🚿🍴🏠

2km North of Coen on the right is a lovely campsite on the Coen River. Please use the toilets as the river flows into Coen and must not be fouled. 21km North of Coen is the Coen airport on the left and just past the airport on the left is Rokeby turnoff. (Rokeby detailed track notes page 137). The rest of the road to Archer River can be quite cut up with long straight sections and winding hilly country (use caution). The Archer River Roadhouse is on the left immediately before the Archer River.

Archer River

Archer River Roadhouse

Archer River Roadhouse is a family owned and operated business. John and Sherrill Mehonoshen are your hosts. The Roadhouse is situated next to the picturesque Archer River, set in landscaped gardens, making it an ideal spot for more than a night's stopover, offering comfortable overnight units.

There is a large camping area with spacious sites all unpowered, showers, toilets and a laundry. Showers are available to non campers for a small fee. The Roadhouse itself has a restaurant where delicious snacks and meals are offered, no one should stop here without trying Sherrill's famous Archer Burger, it's highly recommended and is a meal in itself. Adjacent is a licensed bar in a garden setting for you to enjoy your refreshments, takeaway liquor is available including beer, wine and spirits and ice.

Basic food supplies are available with a large selection of books, souvenirs and maps. In the carpark area is a telephone and fuel station. If you are unfortunate enough to have a mechanical problem, John and Sherrill carry some parts and usually can assist in getting you mobile until you can reach full mechanical services, Coen being the closest. Gas refills are not available.

The Roadhouse is open 7 days a week between 7am – 10pm.

All major credit cards accepted. EFTPOS facilities.

Refuel yourself and your vehicle at the
Archer River Roadhouse

The facilities at the Roadhouse are excellent, and combined with a warm friendly atmosphere it is an ideal stopover to camp or have a break from camping and enjoy the comfortable accommodation with all linen supplied.

For information and bookings contact:

John and Sherrill Mehonoshen
P.M.B. 77
Cairns 4870
Ph:/Fax: 0740 60-3266

NOTE: This is the last fuel stop en route to the Top until Bamaga (approximately 390km). If travelling West, fuel is available at Weipa, approximately 190km, and East, Lockhart River, approximately 140km (fuel at Lockhart River Mon-Fri only). So if travelling North make sure you have enough fuel to Bamaga and any diversions you may make.

Archer River to Wenlock River – 118 km Dirt

20km North of Archer River turn right for Lockhart River, Iron Range, Chili Beach and Portland Roads, otherwise straight ahead for the Top. (Lockhart River, Iron Range, Chili Beach and Portland Roads detailed track notes page 129). 46km from Archer River is the right-hand turn for the Top. Straight ahead for Weipa (detailed track notes for Weipa page 114). Take the right-hand turn here for the Top and at 94km from Archer River on your left is Batavia Airstrip. A left-hand turn here will take you back to Weipa (Weipa detailed track notes page 114). 2km past the Batavia Airstrip a road heads off to the right. This road is called Frenchmans Road and leads to Iron Range, Lockhart River, Portland Roads and Chili Beach (Iron Range, Lockhart River, Portland Roads and Chili Beach detailed track notes page 129). Straight ahead another 20km leads to the Wenlock River. On the North bank of the river on the left is Moreton Station where there is a public telephone. Moreton was part of the historic overland telegraph line and is now open to visitors. It is situated on the northern bank of the Wenlock River just off the main crossing. This area is a great location for bird watchers or naturalists. Facilities at the station include camping, toilet & shower and limited accommodation with meals. There are no food supplies but ice and basic mechanical repairs are available. Day tours can be arranged. For full information contact: Moreton Telegraph Station.

Ph: 0740 60-3360 Fax: 0740 60-3204. **NO FUEL IS AVAILABLE.**

Crossing the Wenlock River at Moreton Station poses no problem with a low river level

Wenlock River to Jardine Ferry – 215km Dirt

27 km North of the Wenlock on your right is Bramwell Station. Road conditions vary from loose sand to corrugated iron stone, watch for dust holes. Just before Bramwell Station on the left is the turnoff to Stones Crossing, to use this road you must have written permission. (See page 128 for details).

Bramwell Station offers limited meals and accommodation, contact: Therese Heinemann – Ph: (0740) 60 3237. 10 km past Bramwell Station you encounter a right hand turn. Here you have a choice of roads:

1 Straight ahead up the Telegraph Track with its many creek crossings and slow going. (detailed track notes page 104).
2 Turn right and travel along the Bypass Road which has no creek crossings and the road is in much better condition.

These roads rejoin each other approximately 43km North of Heathlands. If you wish to travel the Telegraph Track please turn to page 110 for detailed track notes on this section. For continuity only in this section of track notes we will guide you around the Bypass Road. If travelling the Bypass Road be very cautious of the sandy road with its many blind corners and narrow conditions. Turn right here away from the Telegraph Track along the Bypass Road. At the 23km point a right hand turn would take you to Shelburne Bay.

Straight ahead another 35km and on your left is the turnoff to Heathlands Ranger Station. If you intend to camp at Eliot Falls, Captain Billy, Jardine River Crossing or Ussher Point either on your journey up or return you must obtain a camping permit at the Ranger Station. (Heathlands D&O Reserve Page 56) (Shadwell D&O Reserve Page 69) (Jardine National Park information page 66).

Straight ahead 12km and on a sharp left-hand bend in the road on your right is the turnoff to Captain Billy (Captain Billy detailed track notes page 58). Continuing around the left-hand bend and another 45km further on you again meet up with the Telegraph Track coming in from your left. Veer right and travel 10 km to the next intersection.

Decision time again:

1. Straight ahead 6km on the Old Telegraph Track leads you to Eliot Falls and Twin Falls. The road to the falls is quite good, but travelling further along the Old Telegraph Track North from the falls to the Old Jardine River Crossing you encounter some very severe creek crossings with possible winching required (see detailed track notes for this section page (107).
2. Veering left at this intersection takes you along the new and much better Bypass Road to the Jardine Ferry.

For continuity only in this section of track notes we will guide you around the Bypass Road.

Veering left at this intersection along the Bypass Road and at about the 17km mark on your right is a turnoff to the Old Telegraph Track (detailed track notes page 110). Straight ahead for another 7.5kms and on your left is a turnoff to Vrilya Point. A further 3km and on your right is another turnoff to the Old Telegraph Track (detailed track notes page 110). Straight ahead 24km and you are at the Jardine River Ferry Crossing. The ferry operates 7 days a week during daylight hours only (for continuation of track notes turn to page 70).

Jardine Ferry

Jardine Ferry and Injinoo Land Access Fee

Aboriginal traditional lands now cover most of the area north of the Jardine River with the exception of Seisia and Punsand Bay. Communities north of the Jardine are Injinoo, New Mapoon, Umagico and Bamaga.

The Injinoo community are the custodians of the majority of land and on arrival at the ferry you will be charged a fee to traverse and camp on their land. The fee charged covers your return ferry trip, bush camping from the Dulhunty River to the Jardine River (including Bertie Creek, Gunshot Creek, Cockatoo Creek, Sailor Creek and Vrilya Point), access and bush camping at Somerset and the East Coast, Muttee Heads and Jardine River mouth. Your permit also covers fishing access to the Jardine & Jacky Jacky Rivers.

You will also be given a rubbish bag and an Injinoo Handbook, which contains visitor information, full details on all camping sites and community by-laws. We suggest you read this booklet very carefully.

The fee charged is directed towards the upkeep of the ferry service, construction and upgrading of visitor facilities, camping areas, maintenance and rubbish control.

For camping on New Mapoon land Ph: 0740 69-3277. At Umagico there is a camping ground with amenties block and laundry. Ph: 0740 69-3266. Fishing trips from Umagico can be organised by Bob Scott of Jardine Adventures. Ph: 0740 69-3460.

Heathlands Ranger Station

Savo Falls located downstream from Eliot Falls

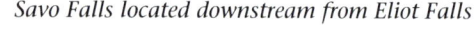

Heathlands D & O Reserve

Heathlands boundaries extend from 5km South of the Dulhunty River in the South, following the telegraph track North to above Eliot Falls, turning East the reserve shares a joint boundary with the Jardine River National Park all the way to the coast. The Southern boundary starting below the Dulhunty River travelling East following the Shelburne Pastoral Holding to the coast. The Eastern coastal boundary is in fact Marine National Park B Zone where fishing and collecting are prohibited, however a portion of coastline at Captain Billy has been left open for recreational fishing out to a 5km coastal limit.

In 1968 the state government granted an occupational licence of some 1140 square miles to Comalco to establish a Pastoral Development in the area to be called Capelands. In conjunction with the C.S.I.R.0. over 4000 acres of land was cleared and sown with 20 different types of grasses and 40 selected legumes were trialled.

In the ensuing years 150 miles of roads were built, a barge ramp was constructed at Captain Billy and numerous buildings, cattle yards and an abattoir were established at outstation No:1 now known as Heathlands. In 1972 fresh beef was supplied to Weipa and Bamaga communities and by 1978 stock numbers had reached some 2000 head. 1985 saw Comalco's withdrawal from Heathlands due to increased financial losses, depressed cattle prices and the remoteness of Heathlands.

This 127,000 hectare property eventually became the Heathlands D & O Reserve. Heathlands is now the National Parks and Wildlife Service Headquarters for Heathlands and Shadwell D & O Reserves along with the Jardine River National Park covering jointly some 366,000 hectares.

Heathlands Reserve is again a very diverse park with rivers and creeks flowing in most directions of the compass. The Western boundary with its rivers flowing into the Gulf are lined with Gallery Forests and open woodlands. Central to the park are the heathlands extending to rainforests on the Great Dividing Range in the East then down the coastal shrubland and thickets covering the coastal sand dunes.

Help preserve flora and fauna by extinguishing all campfires

At the Eastern extremities of the park is Captain Billy Landing, a coastal campsite (no freshwater) with long white beaches interspersed with sand dunes and rocky cliffs. If you intend to travel the road to Captain Billy Landing please call into the Rangers Station at Heathlands first to find out if the road is passable as it is sometimes blocked by fallen trees and large washouts. From the Bypass Road it's a slow 27km (1$\frac{1}{2}$ hours) track into the Landing.

Towards the coast the track to Captain Billy leads across a cliff top before descending to the camp area, the view from here is breathtaking. At the campsite there is a shed you can use for shelter, again here the wind can blow very strongly, we suggest you build fires at the back of the shed where its more sheltered so as to help prevent fires getting out of control with the wind. The coastal area here is spectacular, we suggest a walk along the beach – no vehicles are allowed past the camping area, we found the remains of hatched turtle eggs and the dunes were massed by animal tracks. The animals and birds are in abundance here. Due to Estuarine Crocodiles inhabiting this area, swimming or snorkelling is not recommended. On low tide a walk around the headland is recommended, tide and wind have eroded caves to fascinating shapes – the tide turns again in about 25 minutes so keep an eye out otherwise you will get wet, so it will have to be a quick walk. Again be aware of crocodiles. Fishing is excellent but bait is rather hard to find and fishing from a boat is recommended. There is no restriction on fishing to 5km – out then the area is classed as Marine N.P. "B" Zone, but there are different zonings along this coastline, check your zoning map if unsure (5km limit is out to .5km before the island). We recommend Captain Billy, it certainly is a very scenic spot, the only disadvantages are that the area is susceptible to

Captain Billy Landing

Right: Time and Tides have eroded cliffs into fascinating shapes

The coast North from Captain Billy Landing

Experience superb sunrises from the Camping Ground

The remains of a successful turtle hatching

strong winds and there is very little shade at the camping area and no freshwater.

At the Northern end of the reserve just off the Telegraph Track on the right is a day use only area called Fruitbat Falls, a great spot for a meal and a cooling-off swim.

A few kilometres further North again is the Cape's most renowned campsite, Eliot Falls. The campsite is located at the junction of Eliot Creek and Canal Creek. Just metres upstream from the junction of the Eliot Creek is Eliot Falls and the same distance upstream in Canal Creek from the junction you will find, Twin Falls with crystal-clear water flowing through a series of ponds, making it a great swimming spot for all ages. A short walk down the Eliot Creek brings you to another waterfall known as Savo Falls.

Tropical plants growing along the creek banks in great abundance include the Sundews and Pitcher Plants. A camping permit must be obtained from the Heathlands Ranger Station before camping. Eliot Falls camp is split into three sections: 1. Day use, 2. Overnights, 3. Tour operators, so pay particular attention to the signs when entering the camp.

Toilets have been erected within the park so there is no need to dig your own. Towards the camp's entrance there is a drive-in drive-out rubbish pit where you can dispose of all your rubbish. As this is a well-used camp area there is no firewood left in the immediate area so please gather firewood before entering. Please observe the following:
- Take all rubbish with you if there are no designated rubbish pits.
- Bury all human waste.
- Take extreme care with fire.
- Do not drive vehicles along the beach.
- Be considerate to others.

For further information contact:
The Ranger
Jardine River National Park
Heathlands,
P.M.B. 76 Cairns Mail Centre Qld 4870
Ph: 0740 60-3241

Fruitbat Falls

*Right:
Lush tropical
foliage lines the
banks of the
many creeks
in the area*

Jardine River National Park

The park occupies 237,000 hectares. Its boundaries extend East from the Old Telegraph Line to the coast between the headwaters of the Jardine River in the South and the mangroves of Jacky Jacky Creek and the Escape River in the North.

There is an abundance of water not only in the Jardine River but all through the network of creeks, streams and swamps. The park is dominated by patterns of heathlands, eucalypt forests and rainforests. Areas of swamplands interspersed with Cypress Pines line the many streams and Pitcher Plants can be found along the banks of the creeks. Birds such as Yellow-billed Kingfisher and Fawn-breasted Bowerbirds and Palm Cockatoos have made the park their home and these and many other species will delight birdwatchers.

Access to the coast is at Ussher Point to the North of the National Park. This area along the East coast is adjacent to the Great Barrier Reef Marine Park – Far Northern Section. Marine Park zones have been established to provide a wide range of uses and are similar in concept of National Parks on land, a zoning map will assist with planning fishing trips.

The Jardine National Park is a wilderness, so ensure you have adequate supplies, water, fuel and spare parts, there are none available until Bamaga.

The road that follows the Telegraph Track is the major access to the park. Camping is permitted at Eliot Falls, Jardine River Old Crossing and to the East at Captain Billy Landing and Ussher Point. These areas are under the control of the National Park Ranger, so please plan your trip via Heathlands Ranger Base to get your camping permit even if you intend to camp in these areas on your Southern journey. During your visit to the base you can also obtain various information and advice on travelling this area.

The mighty Jardine River

Previous page: Pristine waters Eliot Falls

Wet Desert – Jardine National Park

NOTE: There is no fuel, supplies or mechanical services at Heathlands Ranger Station.

Please advise the Ranger of any planned walking or hiking trips. National Parks are for everyone's enjoyment but they must be used wisely. So help protect the wilderness value of this park by observing the following:

- Do not disturb plants, animals or landscape. A National Park is an area of total protection.
- Use vehicles only on the main tracks.
- Take extreme care with fire.
- Collect wood en route to camping area, use only fallen wood for campfires.
- If there are no designated rubbish disposal pits, burn and crush rubbish so it is easy to transport.
- Do not use soap or detergent in any stream, river or waterhole.
- Please consider others when using a generator.
- Dig holes and bury human waste if toilets are not provided.
- Fishing is prohibited.
- Firearms are prohibited.
- Pets are not allowed in the park.

For further information contact:
The Ranger
Heathlands
P.M.B. 76,
Cairns Mail Centre 4870
Ph: 0740 60-3241

WARNING: Crocodiles may be present in the creeks, rivers and waterholes and along the beaches of Cape York. Do not swim or prepare food at water's edge or camp within 50m of deep water where these animals may be present.

The Lowlands of Jardine National Park

Shadwell D&O Reserve

The area to the North-East of the Jardine National Park bounded by the Escape River to the coast – an area of some 21,200 hectares – is under the control of the National Parks and Wildlife. The only access to this reserve is via the Ussher Point Road, from the Jardine Ferry, travelling North approximately 14 km and on your right is the turnoff. The track out to Ussher Point (approximately 57km) is very slow and rough with no facilities when you reach the Point. If you intend to camp at Ussher Point you must first obtain a permit from the Rangers Station at Heathlands. Fishing is permitted offshore from Ussher Point.

- Do not disturb plants, animals or landscape. A D&O Reserve is an area of total protection.
- Do not drive vehicles along the beach.
- Use vehicles only on the main tracks.
- Take extreme care with fire.
- Collect wood en route to camping area, use only fallen wood for campfires.
- If there are no designated rubbish disposal pits, burn and crush rubbish so it is easy to transport.
- Do not use soap or detergent in any stream, river or waterhole. * Please consider others when using a generator. * Dig holes and bury human waste if toilets are not provided.
- Fishing is prohibited, except along the coastline (MNP-General use B Zone)
- Firearms are prohibited.
- Pets are not allowed in the park.

For further information contact:
The Ranger
Heathlands
P.M.B. 76,
Cairns Mail Centre 4870
Ph: 0740 60-3241

Button Plant – Dischidia nummularia

Ant House Plant – Myrmecodia beccarii

Jardine Ferry to the Top – 75km

For expanded details and map for North of the Jardine turn to page 75.

Travelling 10km North from the ferry on the Bypass Road, on your right the Old Telegraph Track leads down 4km to the Jardine River. Continuing on the Bypass Road a further 5km and on your right is the turnoff to Ussher Point (page 69). 17km further North you come to a T-junction. Turn right here to the Top. The left-hand track leads to Muttee Heads (page 88). 7km North of this T-junction on your right is the wreckage of a Second World War DC3 aircraft. North 1km T-junction, turn left here. The right-hand road leads to the Bamaga Airport, Jacky Jacky (page 86).

Travelling towards Bamaga and Seisia from this intersection and at the 4.5km mark, turn right for the Top or continue (straight past the turnoff for Bamaga, only 1.5km further on). Turning right here for the Top and travelling 3km a track joins in from the left (this leads back to Bamaga). Continue straight ahead a further 11km past the Lockerbie Scrub and on your right is the Old Lockerbie Homestead. Opposite is the souvenir shop. A track leads off to your left, which leads to Punsand Bay (page 91). Continue straight ahead a further 6.5km, veer left here for the Top (right to Somerset, page 92), and after 3km the track on your left leads to Punsand Bay. Straight ahead 7km and you are at the Pajinka Lodge. Turn left into the carpark and the road straight ahead leads to Pajinka Lodge. The Lodge is owned and operated by the Injinoo community. Activities include field trips, guided fishing tours, birdwatching, night walks, walking and bike-riding trails. For details on accommodation Ph: 1800 802 968. From the carpark it is only a short walk through the rainforest and across the rocks to the most Northerly point of mainland Australia. Day visitors are welcome at Pajinka.

'YES, YOU HAVE MADE IT'

Second World War DC3 aircraft wreckage

Lockerbie Scrub

Cairn located 50 metres from the top of Cape York

Over: Mainland Australia – the most Northerly Point

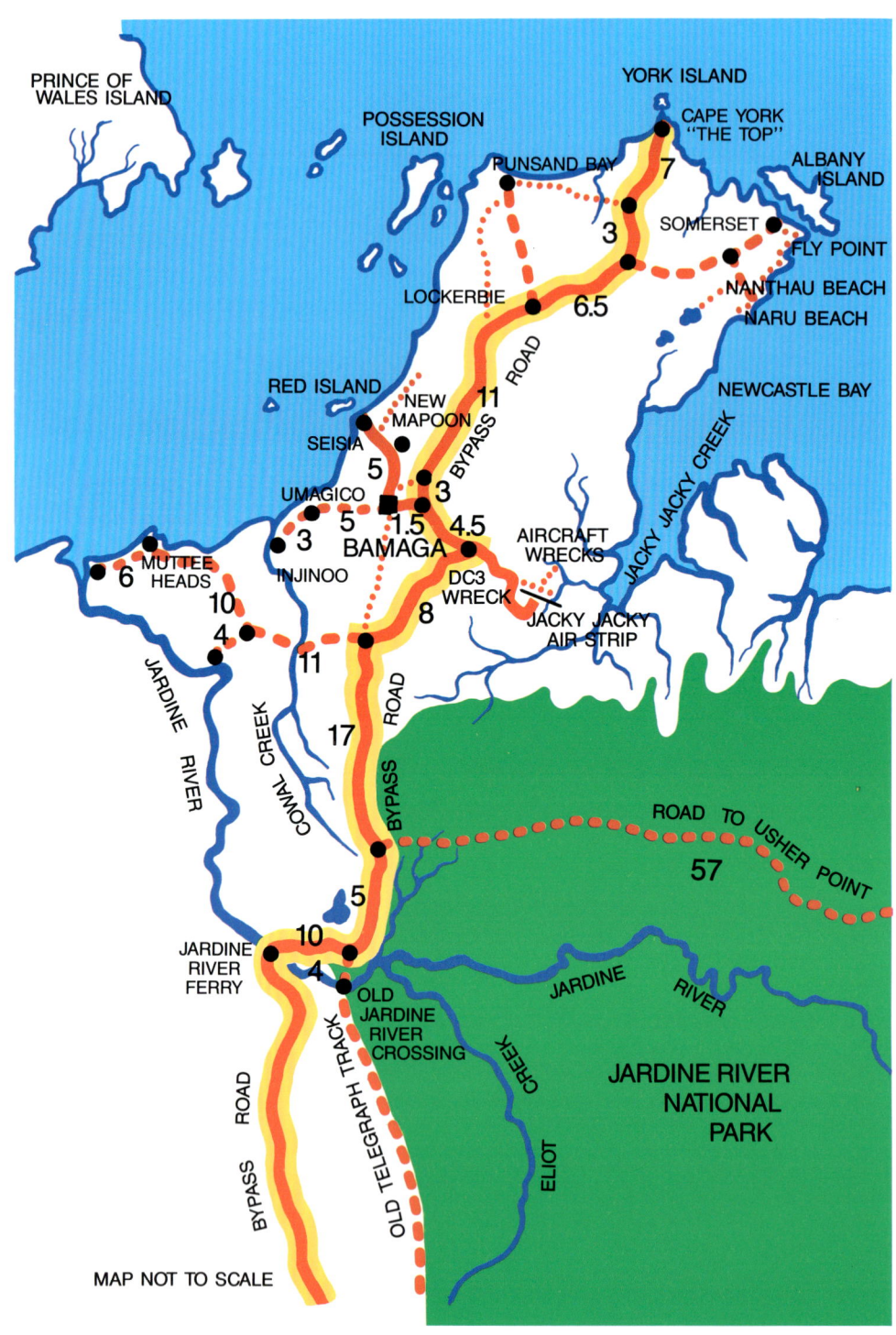

PRINCE OF
WALES ISLAND

POSSESSION
ISLAND

YORK ISLAND

CAPE YORK
"THE TOP"

PUNSAND BAY

7

ALBANY
ISLAND

3

SOMERSET

FLY POINT

LOCKERBIE

6.5

NANTHAU BEACH

NARU BEACH

NEWCASTLE BAY

RED ISLAND

NEW
MAPOON

11

BYPASS ROAD

SEISIA

5

JACKY JACKY CREEK

UMAGICO

5

3

BAMAGA

1.5

4.5

AIRCRAFT
WRECKS

MUTTEE
HEADS

6

3

INJINOO

DC3
WRECK

10

8

4

11

JACKY JACKY
AIR STRIP

JARDINE RIVER

COWAL CREEK

17

ROAD

BYPASS

ROAD TO USHER POINT

57

5

JARDINE
RIVER
FERRY

10

4

OLD
JARDINE
RIVER
CROSSING

JARDINE   RIVER

ELIOT CREEK

JARDINE RIVER
NATIONAL
PARK

BYPASS   ROAD

OLD TELEGRAPH TRACK

MAP NOT TO SCALE

Base mapping supplied by the Department of Lands

NORTH OF THE JARDINE

History of Bamaga and Seisia

The people of Bamaga and Seisia originated from Saibai Island. This island is 24km long and 8km wide and is located 8km off the coast of Papua New Guinea, despite its distance from North Queensland it is still within Queenslands borders. Much of Saibai Island consists of swamplands with some elevated areas containing grasslands. In the wet season these vast swamplands soon become flooded making moving around the island difficult.

After the second world war Saibai was flooded by king tides, Bamaga Ginau the Saibai leader held discussions with his people regarding the problems the island was facing. Erosion was steadily taking place and the island was becoming too small to provide homes for future generations and the availability of enough freshwater was also causing concern. As a result of these discussions chief Bamaga decided it was time to relocate his people.

In 1946 the islanders purchased a lugger from The Department of Native Affairs (DNA) called the "Millard", another lugger the "Mascoy" was also purchased, these vessels would be used to move chief Bamaga's people to Cape York. A temporary site at Muttee Heads was selected for relocation and a decision on the permanent site for the New Settlement would be made later.

The D.N.A. made arrangements for a store and medical post to be built at Muttee Heads, a temporary church would be erected. In June 1947 the first of the families to be relocated set sail on the two luggers to their temporary home. It was very dangerous to travel on luggers as these boats had no engines, but despite the hazards for the rest of 1947 the luggers continued to transport Bamaga's people to Muttee Heads.

Old army huts left over from the war became people's homes and some built their own out of left-over building materials. They soon built a school enabling the children to resume their education, and the community elected a chairman and deputy chairman. With stores being delivered monthly by sea community life was starting to take shape as people started to settle in their temporary home.

Some months later chief Bamaga, the Minister of Lands and some Islanders started to search for a suitable location for a permanent settlement, it was decided that the ideal place would be inland from Red Island Point as there were two creeks in the area which would provide plenty of fresh water for his people.

In February 1949 the Chairman and Deputy Chairman attended a conference on Badu Island to elect Island representatives, at the same time Chief Bamaga was ill in hospital at Thursday Island, he told the chairman he did not have long to live and requested that he and his deputy look after his people. A few days later Chief Bamaga died and the following day his body was moved to Muttee Heads. He was finally buried at Cowal Creek. In May 1949 the land selected by Chief Bamaga was staked out and on the 9th September all the Torres Strait Islanders were invited by the D.N.A. to attend the consecration of the land, during the ceremony they named the land after the Chief "Bamaga". (The Bamaga Show now marks this occasion each September).

During the next 2 years families started to settle in their new area "Bamaga', they built an administration area and houses, but many families returned to Muttee Heads as there was not enough housing. This movement amongst communities continued while the demand for housing was met, but many still stayed in Muttee Heads.

One of the families to travel from Saibai Island was that of Mr Mugai Elu, they settled at Red Island Point and used one of the Army huts to live in. Slowly more families started to settle at Red Island Point and used one of the Army huts to live in. Slowly more families started to settle at Red Island Point and the demand for housing grew, building materials were supplied by the D.N.A. and a village was built. In 1971 they built a church to replace the termporary one, and on 14th October 1972 the church of St Francis of Assisi was dedicated. The people of Red Island Point wanted to change the name of their village, they were asked to wait 5 years – this they did and the name was then changed to Seisia. The name Seisia was formed by taking the first letters of the names of Mr Mugai Elus father and his brothers, they were ***Sagaukaz Elu Isua Sunai Ibuai Aken.***

Bamaga Cemetery – where colourful rituals are performed up to 10 years after the death of a loved one, with the final stage being an official Stone opening

Facilities at Bamaga

Bamaga is the largest community on the Northern Cape with a number of smaller communities in the surrounding area. There is a wide range of facilities here. A service station operates Mon-Fri and Saturday mornings, with limited hours on a Sunday. Mechanical repairs are also available with a good stock of parts being carried. If parts have to be flown in you must be prepared to wait a few days. Ice and gas refills are also available. You can contact the Bamaga Service Station on: 0740 69-3257. Accepted credit cards: Bankcard, Visa, Mastercard.

In the shopping centre there is a souvenir store and a post office where you are welcome to cash your travellers cheques. The supermarket carries a large variety of goods including fresh fruit and vegetables. These are shipped in on a weekly barge, so the freshness will be subject to the barge's arrival. There is also a National Bank Agency within the store. Trading is Mon-Fri and Saturday morning and limited hours on a Sunday. The supermarket has EFTPOS facilities. Telephones are located at the entrance of the shopping centre. Opposite is the canteen where you can purchase beer & wine, no spirits are available. Other facilities in the town include a bakery, ice works and Commonwealth Bank Agency. The Bamaga Motel has twin rooms with meals and is located on Sebasio Street. Ph: 0740 69-3328.

Police - 0740 69-3156
Hospital - 0740 69-3166

Flights from Cairns

Flight West Airlines have flights to Bamaga 5 days a week and charter flights can be organised by Wingz North: 0740 35-9032.

Torres Strait Islanders are experts at fishing

Seisia Today

In 1987 Joseph Elu, the son of Mugai Elu, was elected chairman of the Seisia Island Council. Joseph Elu realised the potential of the Seisia District and the value of its location and has embarked on some enterprising ventures. The existing camping ground was upgraded and a kiosk installed, and traditional island dancing was introduced to entertain the visitors.

The camping ground office is working towards being the most comprehensive "Visitor Information Centre" in the area, enabling the visitor to obtain the most from their stay in Seisia. The aim of the Seisa Island Council is to make Seisia the "Gateway to the Torres Strait". The facilities in the community are now excellent, the council having completed the new wharf, service station, on site accommodation and supermarket. The Seisia Island Council and community are striving towards being totally self-sufficient, and judging by the progress being made they will achieve this, making Seisia an exciting holiday destination for visitors to Cape York.

The palm fringed foreshore at Seisia Camping Ground

Traditional Island Dancing

During the height of the tourist season, traditional island dancing is conducted on special occasions. Contact the Seisia Camping Ground for details.

Fully armed warriors engage in mock battles, portraying their culture through dance and movement. These performances are really spectacular and provide a great evening's entertainment for all the family. Contact the camping ground office for details.

FACILITIES – Seisia Camping Ground

The camping ground is the most centrally located camping area situated on the most sheltered length of coastline at the top of Australia. There are two beachfront camping areas fringed by coconut palms overlooking the islands of Torres Strait. Hot and cold showers and laundry facilities are within easy walking distance of all campsites. Some campsites have shelters with their own kitchens for easy family camping.

Accommodation is also available at the Seisia Seaview Lodge adjacent to the camping area. These twin-share comfortable units are serviced daily and have a fully equipped communal kitchen, barbecue area and laundry facilities. There is a restaurant and kiosk located within the camping ground. Here you can eat in or select from an impressive menue of takeaway food. A large range of groceries is available along with ice cream, soft drinks and party ice. Freshly baked bread is generally available daily. All information on the area can be obtained from the Seisia Camping Ground Office. This "Information Centre" provides the visitor with all up-to-date information on the area's facilities and attractions including information on birdwatching, fishing trips, cruises, boat and trailer hire and motorcycle tours. A wide range of souvenirs and artifacts from the islands of the Torres Strait is also available.

The Seisia Camping Ground is the most centrally located base for touring the Cape. It offers the opportunity for travellers to leave their camp in one place while they tour both North-East to the Top and South-West to the mouth of the Jardine and has the most comprehensive information centre in the area. For all enquiries contact: Seisia Camping Ground, 0740 69-3243 or 0740 69-3155.

EFTPOS facilities. Seisa Kiosk 0740 69-3285.

Late evening fishing from the Seisia Jetty

TOURS TO BE TAKEN

Thursday Island

A direct ferry service operates each day from Seisia wharf departing at 8am. Visitors have 5 hours on the island including a $1^1/_2$ hour tour of the island. Bookings for the ferry can be made at the camping ground office.

Fishing

The coastline North and South of Seisia wharf is the most sheltered on the Cape, making it the safest place for inshore boating. Seisia has the only concrete boat ramp North of the Jardine. There is another launching ramp 20 minutes away at the Jacky Jacky estuary, which is the second-largest and most pristine mangrove estuary in Australia. The office provides a low-cost fishing map on how and where to catch barramundi and other tropical sports fish, plus a wide range of fishing tackle and bait to satisfy any angler's need.

Hire boats are available for $^1/_2$ and full days. No licence is required for smaller boats with outboard motors less than 6hp. The wharf at Seisia is one of the best land-based fishing spots on Cape York, where an abundance of fish are found under the jetty. It is also a great place to meet fellow travellers and the local community.

Alternatively there are both day and extended guided fishing tours to the Jardine River and Jacky Jacky estuary for barramundi and other sports fish.

FISHING SAFARI PACKAGES

Gary Wright's Wilderness Safaris offers both day & extended guided fishing tours. Accommodation packages can be arranged to suit your individual needs. For further information contact: Gary Wright, 0740 69-3400.

Cape York Rod & Rifle Safaris also offers both day & extended fishing tours. Pig-hunting tours can also be arranged with rifle & bow hunters catered for. For further information contact: Ian and Rachel McConnell, Ph/Fax: 0740 69-3467.

ADDITIONAL FACILITIES

The Seisia Service Station is open 7 days with all fuels and oils available for your vehicle. All major credit cards accepted. AMPOL

The Seisia Supermarket located in the village carries a wide range of groceries and fresh produce at very competitive prices.

Hire Cars

Steven and Elsie Nawia operate Seisia Hire Cars. Late-model 4WDs are available for daily or weekly hire. For visitors wishing to explore the area North of the Jardine only, you can fly to Bamaga and pre-arrange a hire vehicle.

Contact: Steven and Elsie Nawia

Ph: 0740 69-3368 or 0740 69-3289 for current rates and availability.

Taxi

The Bamaga and district taxi service provides transport to all area North of the Jardine. Advanced bookings are necessary for extended trips to Cape York and Somerset and for airport arrivals – Contact: 0740 69-3333. A/H: 0740 69-3400. Next-door to the taxi office is a laundromat.

Barging Services

If you experience serious mechanical problems or have no desire to travel back to Cairns by road, you can barge your vehicle or motorbike on the weekly service to Cairns. For more details on this service contact the camping ground.

Mechanical Assistance

Top End Motors operated by Eric Gurousk in Seisia offers specialised mechanical repair work for 4WD vehicles. A small range of spare parts is available along with battery and tyre repairs. If spare parts have to be flown in from Cairns you will have to wait a few days, depending on the availability of parts. Parts from interstate will take longer – contact:

Top End Motors
Tradesman Way, Seisia
Bamaga 4876. Ph: 0740 69-3182. A/H 0740 69-3135.

Welding

Top Form Engineering provide welding repairs on everything from radiators to roof racks. They also specialise in motor vehicle and trailer suspension repairs. Outboard motors and boats can also be repaired and a small amount of ships chandlery is available. Bottle gas refills are also available.

Contact: Bob & Evelyn Mitchell
Top Form Engineering
Tradesman Way, Seisia.
Ph: 0740 69-3230. Fax: 0740 69-3326.

Air Services

Daily flights from Cairns are to nearby Bamaga. Flights north to the islands of the Torres Strait can also be arranged. Enquire at the camping ground office.

Display of Second World War aircraft engines in Bamaga

Tranquil sunsets at Seisia

Fishing Tackle Shop

A short distance from the Seisia Jetty is Gebadi's Tackle Shop. For all your fishing tackle and bait requirements contact: Edna Gebadi's Tackle Shop. Ph: 0740 69-3279.

Seisia is the gateway to the Torres Strait, and it has something to offer for everyone. It is ideal for families, with plenty of room for children. The spacious campsites are perfect for Tag-A Long Tours, enabling groups to all camp in one area, and is the perfect location to base yourself. We thoroughly recommend a visit to Seisia. The facilities and services offered are excellent and it is a must for all visitors.

Second World War Relics

During the Second World War Cape York was used extensively by all our armed forces as a departure point for our war effort. Many reminders of this conflict are still located throughout the region, even though they are largely overgrown and rather hard to recognise.

Over the years many of our war veterans have returned to the Cape to look over the areas where they and their mates served their country in time of conflict. An airfield was constructed at Bamaga during the Second World War, originally named Higginsfield after an American serviceman, but was changed after the war to honour the faithful companion of Edmund Kennedy "Jacky Jacky". A plaque has been erected at the airport dedicating the airstrip to him. The airport now serves all the local community and resorts up North and regular passenger flights operate daily. Still located around the airstrip are the old aircraft taxiways leading well into the surrounding bush, still littered with hundreds of overgrown and rusting refuelling drums.

The most noticeable war relic in the area is the DC 3 located on the main road lkm before the Bamaga, Jacky Jacky airport T-intersection. This aircraft crashed on May 5th 1945 with the loss of 6 lives. This site and two other sites are now fenced and are dedicated memorials to their crew and passengers. There are also two aircraft wrecks located in the bush adjacent to the Northern end of the airstrip. These are located by driving from the Main road – Airport intersection, approximately 2km as the road bears right towards airport, turn immediate left and you will see a gate, drive through and please leave gate as you find it. Drive lkm, track bears left, on your left is the first wreck that of a downed Hurricane. lkm further, drive up left track for short distance to 2nd wreck – Beaufort Bomber. Both these areas are also memorials to the pilots and crew so please keep outside the fenced area.

Rusting memories of the Second World War

Silent memorials to our brave
Second World War pilots

One of the more unusual relics of the war years is located just past Muttee Heads on Radar Hill. A 15-metre radar tower is still standing in all its glory, poised ready to scan the seas of Torres Strait and skies above. Just below the tower are still some of the trenches and rock fortifications used during the war.

Travelling past Muttee Heads on the way to the mouth of the Jardine River you cross over a grid on the quarantine fence. Veering right over the grid and following the fence along about 300 metres, looking to your right past the fence and up the hill, the radar tower is located partially hidden in the trees at the top of the hill.

A word of warning to people who may consider fossicking around these old Second World War sites, that they are still a protected area and heavy fines are imposed on anyone found removing articles. Metal detectors are totally forbidden as there is still live ammunition in a very unstable and explosive condition scattered right throughout the area.

Muttee Heads

88

Second World War radar tower at Muttee Heads

Mouth of the Jardine River

Punsand Bay with the tip of Cape York in the distance

Punsand Bay Private Reserve

Punsand Bay Safari and Fishing Lodge is just 7km from the tip of Cape York and is an ideal base to explore the tip. Your hosts maintain the beautiful beachfront camping area, which boasts all modern amenities including hot showers, toilets and coin-operated laundry. There are a limited number of beachfront tents and basic cabin-style rooms with semi ensuite facilities and verandahs overlooking the Torres Strait. All linen is supplied and both styles of accommodation are serviced daily. Accommodation packages including meals are available. Three meals are served daily in the covered, open-air, licensed dining room and bar, which is open to all visitors.

Punsand Bay is centrally located to all attractions, making touring easy. The Thursday Island ferry departs daily (except Sunday) from the beach, and there are a number of self-guided bush walks and full-day barramundi and Blue Water fishing safaris to choose from. Informative slide shows feature just a few of the other activities available.

Other facilities include basic food items, ice, souvenirs and mechanical repairs. NO FUEL IS AVAILABLE.

For information and bookings contact Punsand Bay Safari Lodge, Bamaga, Queensland 4876 Ph: 0740 69-1722. Fax: 0740 69-1403.

Somerset and the Jardines

For many years there was talk of establishing a settlement at the tip of Cape York. In 1863 a government residency was built at Somerset. In July 1864, Captain John Jardine, a police magistrate from Rockhampton, arrived by ship to Somerset Bay to take up his position as Government Resident Captain and to establish settlement of Somerset. Accompanying him was suitable qualified personnel to accomplish this task. Seeing the need to be self sufficient in this remote area, Jardine obtained permission from The Colonial Government to herd cattle and horses overland, Captain Jardine's two eldest sons Frank and Alec would head the team on the drive. On 11th October 1864 they set out from Carpentaria Downs Station near Rockhampton with 250 head of cattle and 41 horses, the trip was to take 4 months, it in fact took over 5 months, the party had to endure great hardship with the inhospitable terrain. Their maps were inaccurate and they had many an encounter with hostile aborigines. It proved to be one of the most incredible tests of endurance recorded in Australian exploration. Frank and Alec finally arrived at Somerset on 2nd March 1865 with the other members of the party and remaining stock being escorted in a few days later.

Captain John Jardine having completed establishing the settlement returned to Rockhampton in December 1865 to resume his duties as Magistrate, a Captain Henry Simpson took over the Government Residency, but ill health forced him to retire. Frank Jardine was offered and accepted the position in 1868 as the new magistrate at Somerset.

In recognition of his trek overland with the cattle, Frank Jardine was granted grazing land West of Somerset, the property was named "Lockerbie".

Early in 1873 Frank met and fell in love with a Samoan Princess Sana Solia, she was the niece of the King of Samoa. They were married at Somerset in October that year, they left Somerset for Mt Ernest Island in Torres Strait to pursue pearling and copra interests. In 1877 the residency at Somerset was abandoned with the administration being transferred to Thursday Island. Frank and Sana returned to Somerset and raised their family, Frank kept his interests in cattle but pearling was his main interest.

Frank Jardine died in 1919, with Sana passing away in 1923, both were buried on the foreshore below the residency. Frank's eldest son rebuilt the Somerset residency which had deteriorated over the years, but saw no future for Somerset and departed for the Dutch East Indies. (Somerset was leased out, but the onset of the war caused evacuations from the area and enlistments for the men, so Somerset was finally abandoned). Soldiers in the area finding the place deserted took many items from the homestead and over the years the property deteriorated and eventually was destroyed by fire in 1960, a sad end to a fine old homestead.

Information derived from the book: The Holland Family
Lockerbie, Cape York
By A.M. Hall

Somerset today

There's not much left of the old homestead now, only a few relics lie around to remind us of bygone years, but as you stroll around the property you can't help imagining what life must have been like. The views would have been breathtaking, but the tall vegetation now blocks these views of Albany Island and the Passage. Please help to preserve this area and do not remove anything from the site. On the left just before Somerset is a track leading down to the beach and the Jardine graves, it's fairly steep but poses no problems if you take your time, this is an excellent picnic spot, but no camping is allowed. Access to the graves is by walking left along the beach where they can be located about 100 metres from the Northern end.

At the Southern end of the beach the track takes you alongside the mangroves where good birdlife can be found. A short distance further on the right is an old well that was part of the Jardine days, this water is totally unsuitable for humans and should not be touched.

The last resting place of Frank Jardine

Looking up the hill from the beach to the Old Somerset Homestead Site

Entrance to the remains of the Somerset Homestead

East Coast Beaches

The east coast section from Fly Point south to Nanthau Headland is under a strict revegetation program initiated by the Injinoo Council, with certain sections and beaches closed and access limited to specific areas. At present access to the two southern beaches of the east coast are open to the public for day visits and for the first time camping is also allowed. The three northern beaches are at present closed to the public for regeneration but access to Fly Point from Somerset is still open.

A freshwater soak is located on the first beach with campsites located higher on the beaches so please watch the high tide mark.

On the track out to the beaches on the right is a small trail leading to the freshwater Lake Boronto. As this is a very pristine area we suggest you leave your car just off the main track and take a short walk to the lake through the sprawling vegetation interspersed with numerous variates of wild flowers.

When reaching the lake be cautious of crocodiles. Whilst we saw no signs of their presence it certainly is the right environment for them.

For the latest information on this area please refer to your Injinoo handbook.

The coastal track along Freshwater Bay

95

Aboriginal middens are scattered along the bay as shown in the right of the picture

Aboriginal middens

Lush rainforest extends right to the tip of Cape York

The rainforest supports many varieties of tropical plants

Red Berry – Syzygium fibrosum (fruit)

Torres Strait

The Torres Strait Islanders have a long and colourful history. Well-established trade routes existed for hundreds of years before European settlement, and the Spaniards, Portuguese and Dutch sailed through the area long before Captain Cook's passage in 1770. The many islands had their own societies, but violence dominated much of this area with cannibalism and head-hunting being rife. In the 1820's Trepangers were the first Europeans to spend any length of time in the area. They made their way from Sydney in their cutters collecting sea cucumbers (bêche-de-mer), which they sold to Asia. The main influx of foreigners came in 1868 with the discovery of the pearl shell. Men came from all over the Pacific in search of this gem. Unfortunately the pearl caused a lot of fights and killings amongst the boat crews and havoc was caused on all the islands. To maintain some stability in the area the London Missionary Society was encouraged by Frank Jardine to come to the islands to establish a mission. This they did, and in 1871 they arrived at Darnley Island. This occasion is now celebrated annually on July 1st in a festival called "The Coming of the Light". There was plenty of work for the missionaries and other missions were soon established on surrounding islands.

The pearling industry flourished, but recruits for the pearling boats did not always work of their own free will. In 1877 the Government moved its official residence and Police Magistrate from Somerset to Thursday Island, and in 1879 all of the Strait's islands came under Queensland control. By 1890 nearly 300 pearling boats were operating from Thursday Island. Over the years Japanese divers and skippers dominated the industry, but it was a dangerous profession and many of them died of the bends. In 1914 the London Missionary Society handed over their involvement to the Anglican Church. World War 2 had a significant effect on the Torres Strait. Many islanders joined up, all civilians were evacuated and the Japanese people were interned in Southern Australia. On the 14th March 1942 the Horn Island Air Base was bombed with a number of other raids following, but Thursday Island was spared.

After the war the price of pearls went up, but with the introduction of plastics it did not last long and in 1960 the Japanese introduced their method of "seeding" live shells. Cultured pearl stations were established and in the 1970's the pearling industry based around Thursday Island was worth over a million dollars. Today only a few boats work the area, as the pearl is scarce. A Japanese company still operates a pearl farm on Albany Island. A gold mine on Horn Island, which commenced operations in 1988, has now closed down.

Tourism is slowly increasing as Thursday Island becomes a popular destination for Cape travellers.

There are approximately 15 islands in the Torres Strait group, with the population made up of various nationalities including Japanese, Chinese, Filipino, Malay, Aboriginal and European. Although a lot of the original culture has disappeared, traditional singing, dancing and crafts are still practised throughout the area.

Access to Thursday Island

Peddells Ferry Service operates a regular passenger service from Bamaga to Thursday Island. Ph: 0740 69-1551. Sunstate Airlines and Flight West have regular flights to Horn Island (Thursday Island Airport). Charter flights can be organised with Wingz North – Ph: 0740 35-9032. Several barges service the island taking passengers as well as freight – contact:

Jardine Shipping.
Ph: 0740 35 1900
Seaswift on: 0740 35 1234

Guns at Green Hill Fortress

Thursday Island with Prince of Wales Island in the background

Facilities

There are a number of general stores, a chemist, a newsagent and takeaway food outlets. Counter meals are also available at the island's 4 hotels. There is a shopping centre with a large supermarket, and for banking requirements there is a National Bank and a Post Office.

Accommodation – There are no camping facilities on Thursday Island.

Federal Hotel	Victoria Pde	Ph: 0740 69-1569
Grand Hotel	Victoria Pde	Ph: 0740 69-1557
Royal Hotel	Douglas St.	Ph: 0740 69-1537
Torres Strait Hotel	Douglas St.	Ph: 0740 69-1141
Rainbow Motel	Douglas St.	Ph: 0740 69-2460
Jardine Motel	Cnr Normanby St./Victoria Pde.	Ph: 0740 69-2555
Mura Mudh Hostel	Douglas Street	Ph/Fax: 0740 69-2050

Tours around the Island

There are two companies operating a bus tour around the island. The round trip takes approximately 1½ hours, and during that time there's a full commentary explaining the fascinating history of this area. Some of the highlights include a visit to the Green Hill Fortress, the Thursday Island Cemetery, where colourful memorials to Japanese pearl divers are housed, beautiful old churches and colonial buildings. For further details contact:

Peddells Ferry & Tour Bus Service
P.O. Box 65,
Thursday Island.
Qld. 4875.
Phone: 0740 69-1551
Fax: 0740 69-1365

Emergency Numbers:
Police: 0740 69-1520
Hospital: 0740 69-1109

Customs House – Thursday Island

One of the many well kept churches on Thursday Island

Plaque on Possession Island where Lt. Captain James Cook claimed possession of New Holland for Great Britain in 1770

Jardine Motel – Thursday Island

Jardine Motel

Located on Thursday Island's beachfront is the three-star Jardine Motel. This tropically designed two-storey motel boasts breathtaking views across the Strait. One of the special features of this complex is the display of artworks by local islanders, with their colourful paintings depicting their culture and beliefs. The motel offers 37 modern rooms, all with private facilities including airconditioning, T.V., radio, telephone, with access to a facsimile machine.

Specialities of the licensed restaurant in the complex include locally caught crayfish and coral trout plus a large range of other tempting meals to choose from. As you relax by the pool you can sample one of many local exotic drinks that are available from the bar, or for the more energetic take one of the many tours that are offered. Fishing and diving trips are available and excursions to surrounding islands can be arranged. The Jardine Motel, set in landscaped gardens, is Thursday Island's most luxurious accommodation, offering all the comforts of home combined with a Torres Strait atmosphere, and is the perfect location to relax after the hot, dusty roads of the Cape.

For enquiries and bookings contact:
Jardine Motel
Cnr Normanby St. & Victoria Pde.
Thursday Island
Ph: 0740 69-2555
Fax: 0740 69-1470
All major credit cards accepted and Australian travellers cheques.

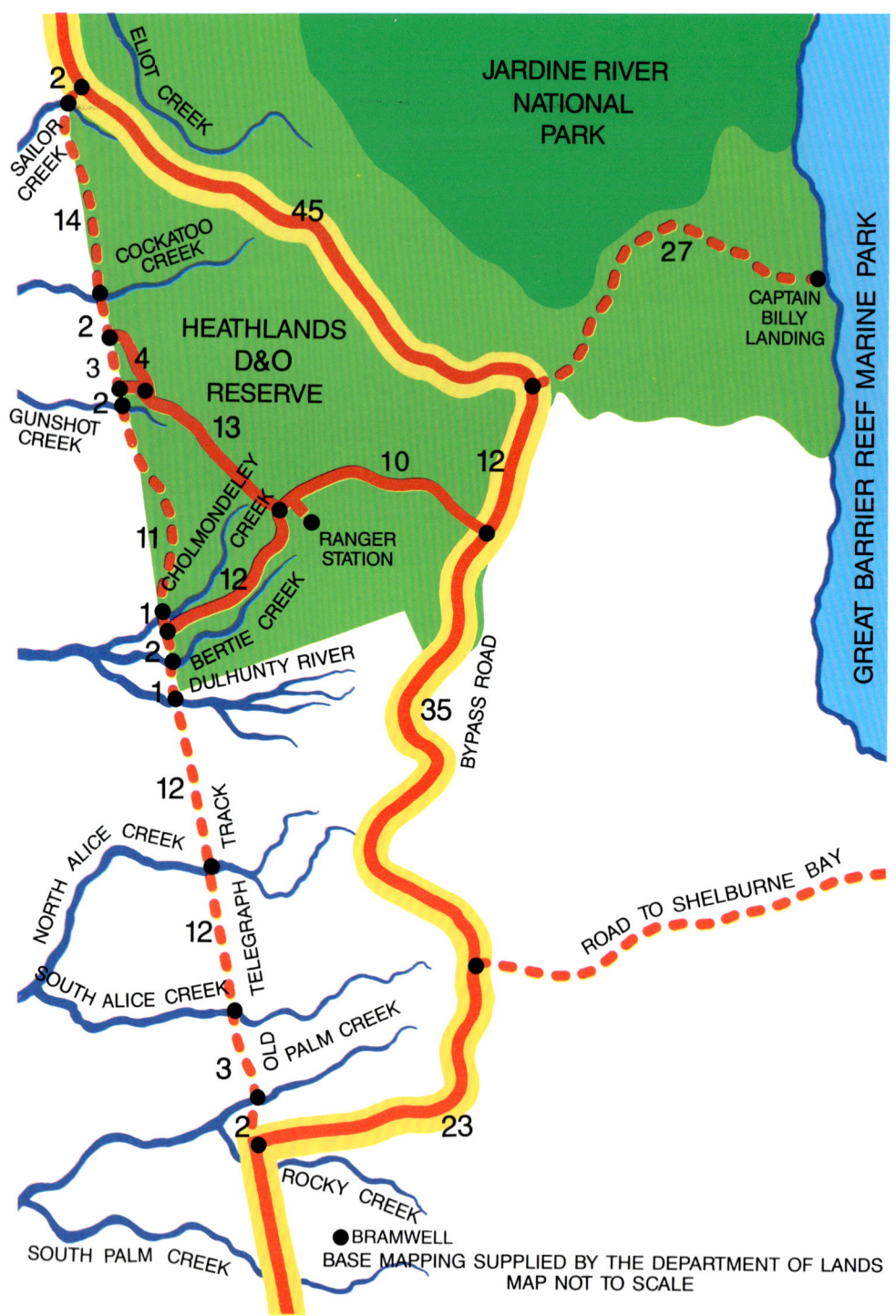

JARDINE RIVER
NATIONAL
PARK

ELIOT CREEK

SAILOR CREEK

2

14

COCKATOO CREEK

2

3   4

2

GUNSHOT CREEK

HEATHLANDS
D&O
RESERVE

13

11

CHOLMONDELEY CREEK

12

1

2

BERTIE CREEK

1

DULHUNTY RIVER

45

27

CAPTAIN
BILLY
LANDING

GREAT BARRIER REEF MARINE PARK

10

12

RANGER
STATION

BYPASS ROAD

35

12

NORTH ALICE CREEK

TELEGRAPH TRACK

12

SOUTH ALICE CREEK

ROAD TO SHELBURNE BAY

3

OLD PALM CREEK

2

23

ROCKY CREEK

SOUTH PALM CREEK

BRAMWELL

BASE MAPPING SUPPLIED BY THE DEPARTMENT OF LANDS
MAP NOT TO SCALE

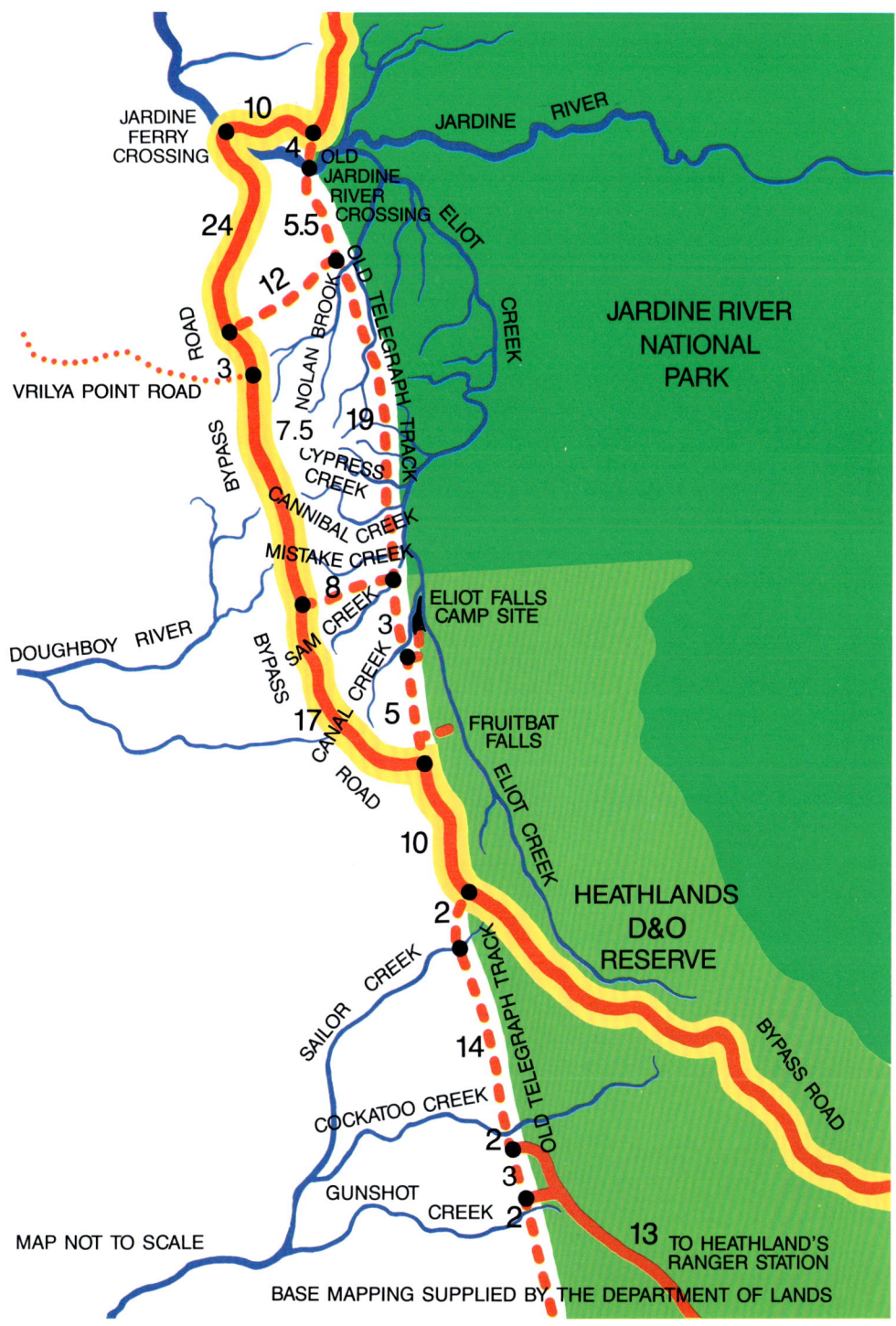

JARDINE FERRY CROSSING

10

4 OLD JARDINE RIVER CROSSING

JARDINE RIVER

ELIOT CREEK

JARDINE RIVER NATIONAL PARK

24

5.5

12

ROAD

VRILYA POINT ROAD

3

OLD TELEGRAPH TRACK

NOLAN BROOK

7.5

19

CYPRESS CREEK

BYPASS

CANNIBAL CREEK

MISTAKE CREEK

DOUGHBOY RIVER

8

SAM CREEK

3

ELIOT FALLS CAMP SITE

BYPASS

CANAL CREEK ROAD

17

5

FRUITBAT FALLS

ELIOT CREEK

10

HEATHLANDS D&O RESERVE

2

SAILOR CREEK

OLD TELEGRAPH TRACK

14

BYPASS ROAD

COCKATOO CREEK

2

3

GUNSHOT CREEK

2

13 TO HEATHLAND'S RANGER STATION

MAP NOT TO SCALE

BASE MAPPING SUPPLIED BY THE DEPARTMENT OF LANDS

Bramwell to Old Jardine River Crossing via the Old Telegraph Track or Heathlands

13km North of Bramwell Station there is the road junction of the Old Telegraph Track and the Bypass Road. A right-hand turn here takes you along the Bypass Road (for detailed track notes of the Bypass Road turn to page 54).

Travelling the Old Telegraph Track with its many creek crossings and good camp spots can be one of the most rewarding tracks on the Cape. Be warned that on this section of the track you will find the most severe creek crossing on the Cape – "Gunshot" – with its quarry-like South Bank. Only attempt Gunshot and the following creek, Cockatoo Creek, with its very sandy Northern bank, if you have a winch with you. You can still travel the first section of the Telegraph Track with its less severe creek crossings and turn off 2km past Bertie Creek, travelling via Heathlands Ranger Station to the Bypass Road.

It is not our intention to describe each creek crossing or the road's condition in detail as these change each year with the wet season and the amount of usage that the track is subjected to. As the track is not maintained it is rough and in parts rocky, with many washouts along the way, so drive cautiously. Early in the season soon after the wet many of the dips can be filled with water and these can become very soft. Walk all creek crossings first and choose your entrance and exit points.

If you have reached a creek crossing and are unsure whether you have the ability or experience to tackle it you have two choices.

1. Let some other more experienced motorist tackle it first then assess the situation after he has crossed.

2. Look at the map to find a detour and back track.

MOST IMPORTANTLY – Do not be bullied into any situation on the track which you feel that you cannot handle with confidence, remembering that you are miles from any medical or mechanical assistance.

Gunshot Crossing – The Choice is Yours

Crossing Bertie Creek

Travelling North 2km along the Telegraph Track from the Bypass Junction the first creek you cross is Palm Creek, followed 3km further on by South Alice Creek. Another 12km further on you cross the North Alice Creek with only 12km to the Dulhunty. At the Dulhunty there is good water for swimming and camping. 1km North of the Dulhunty is Bertie Creek with its solid rock bottom and very large and deep holes at the crossing – use caution.

2km North of Bertie Creek on the right is the turnoff to Heathlands Ranger Station and the Gunshot Creek Crossing Detour. If you don't want to attempt the Gunshot Creek Crossing but still want to have a look at it we suggest you detour here and travel up through Heathlands then rejoin the track 2km North of the Gunshot Crossing.

If you intend to camp at either Eliot Falls, Old Jardine River Crossing, Captain Billy Landing or Ussher Point you can call into the Ranger Station and obtain your permits on this detour. When rejoining the Telegraph Track after the Heathlands detour, turn left (South) 2km and you are at the Gunshot Creek Crossing, or as we like to call it, a quarry.

Gunshot Creek Crossing

There are four approaches on the Southern bank, each ending in muddy water holes at the bottom. The Choice Is Yours. Some of the incidents that have occurred to travellers while trying to negotiate Gunshot include, roof racks and contents landing in front of the car, boats landing the wrong way up in the creek, vehicle contents landing on the bonnet intermixed with parts of the windscreen, and the most common one happens at the bottom of the bank when the fan becomes part of the radiator.

After the condition of the Southern bank the Northern bank doesn't even rate a mention except that there is a camp area with a shelter. The approaches to Gunshot Creek change annually.

Gunshot – Going . . .

. . . Going

. . . Gone

Travelling North from Gunshot (if you can) at 2km a track on your right leads to Heathlands Ranger Station and if intending to camp at Eliot Falls, Old Jardine River Crossing, Captain Billy Landing or at Ussher Point you must call in and obtain your permit.

Travelling North another 5km from this junction you are at the approach to Cockatoo Creek. The creek crossing has a firm rock base with large erosion holes and a very long and sandy uphill Northern bank. If you have to winch yourself up the Northern bank please use a tree guard around the tree at the top of the climb. Don't be like previous unthinking travellers and just wrap your winch cable around the tree's base in time ringbarking and killing it. There are good campsites on both banks but remember please don't litter.

From Cockatoo Creek to Sailor Creek is 14km, with two approaches on the Southern bank so check it out before driving through. 2km North of Sailor Creek coming in from your right is the Bypass Road. Travelling another 10km North from this junction you are confronted with another choice of tracks.

Turning left here takes you along the Bypass track – 51km to the Jardine Ferry Crossing (for detailed track notes turn to page 55). Travelling straight ahead North along the Old Telegraph Track are some of the Cape's most pristine creeks and waterfalls.

The road into Fruitbat and Eliot Falls is quite easy to negotiate but after Eliot Falls the road again traverses some difficult creek crossings where winching maybe required.

Cockatoo Creek

Travelling North up the Old Telegraph Track l00m is the turnoff to Fruitbat Falls on your right (picnic area only). Straight ahead you cross Scrubby Creek and after a further 5km you are at the Eliot Falls turnoff on your right with its top swimming and camping 1.5km down this track.

The track North from Eliot Falls turnoff, all the creeks from here to the Old Jardine Road Crossing have exceptionally crystal clear water, appearing only to be millimetres deep but in walking each crossing you will find the water to be inexcess of a metre deep in places.

PLEASE WALK ALL CREEK CROSSINGS.

Travelling North from the Eliot Falls turnoff there are three ways of getting back onto the Bypass track.

1. Cross Canal and Sam Creek then turn left back to the Bypass track South of the Ferry Crossing (quite easy).
2. Cross all the creeks turning left after Nolan Brook back to the Bypass track South of the Ferry Crossing (winching may be required).
3. Crossing all creeks and fording the Jardine River meeting up with the Bypass track North of the Ferry Crossing (winching may be required).

Downstream from Sam Creek Crossing

Above, left and right: Spoon Leaf Sundew – Drosera spathulata

Pitcher Plants – Nepenthes mirabilis

Travelling North from the Eliot Falls turnoff about 100 metres the first creek crossing is Canal Creek. Check the creek for holes and inspect the Northern bank for your exit up through the springs and washouts. 3km past Canal Creek is Sam Creek which is a rather easy crossing but beware of holes in the creek bed.

There is a small campsite on the Northern bank of Sam Creek. 1.6km North of Sam Creek on your left is the first turnoff back to the Bypass track. The creek crossings North of this turnoff should not be attempted unless you have a winch.

Continuing North the only creek to have a bridge across it is Cypress and this bush bridge is narrow so use caution. All the approaches and exits of the creeks, Mistake, Cannibal, Logan and Nolan Brook change each year with the wet season and the amount of traffic using the road. The banks are the hardest part to negotiate with actual water section quite easy. Remember when you exit the creek the underside and tyres of your vehicle are wet and this leads to traction problems as you try to climb up the bank on your exit from the creek.

Cannibal Creek

Fording Nolan Brook

Winching up the Southern Bank of Nolan Brook

Walk all the creek crossings and pay particular attention to the exit route to be taken, especially the upper top sandy sections. When walking Cannibal Creek keep a good check on the upstream tyre track as there is a hidden spring hole about 10 metres from the Northern bank. Nolan Brook had a bush bridge crossing until it was burnt out in 1990 and now the crossing has a very steep Southern bank, but quite an easy Northern bank. In 1991, towards the end of the season, we actually had to winch ourselves up the Southern bank of Nolan Brook through the sand at the top of Cannibal Creek, so if you intend travelling this section of the track please take a winch with you.

2km North of Nolan Brook there is a track on your left that leads back to the Bypass track South of the Jardine Ferry. This is the track you must take unless you intend fording the Jardine at the Old River Crossing.

Continuing North at this intersection for another 5.5km veering slightly right you are at the Jardine River and the many tracks in this area. Downstream you will find the Old Telegraph Line Crossing, and upstream for those wishing to drive across is the vehicle ford. Please use caution when camping at or crossing the Jardine River as it is inhabited with Estuarine Crocodiles.

If intending to ford the Jardine (160 metres), consider a few things first, such as: is your winch cable long enough to reach to a good anchor point? are your vehicle's electrics waterproofed? is your vehicle's engine air intake above the water level and bow wave?

DO NOT STOP IN THE MIDDLE OF THE RIVER

As the Jardine has a sand base at the crossing, if you happen to stop midstream the current washes the sand away from around and under your tyres, giving you and your vehicle that sinking feeling.

Old Jardine River Crossing

Archer River to Weipa — 181km 🛏️🚿🍴🛏️🏠✂️➕

46km north of Archer River is the right hand turn for the top. Straight ahead for Weipa. 34km further along the Weipa Road is the left hand turn to Aurukun Aboriginal Settlement, continue straight ahead 12km and on your left again is the second road leading back down to the Aurukun Aboriginal Settlement, continue North for 24km and on your right is the road that leads back to the Telegraph Track at Batavia. Straight past this turnoff you have 65km of good road into Weipa. At the sight of the first mine clearing on this road please turn to page 116 for the map of Weipa and instructions as to the no access areas.

Batavia to Weipa — 105km

Please use extreme caution along this track as it's quite heavily stocked with cattle and the track can become quite boggy after rain with the creek crossings becoming impassable.

Travelling West alongside the Batavia Airstrip, down past the homestead with the road leading through some very lush country. At the 40km intersection you are at the main Weipa – Archer River road. Turn right to Weipa 65km or left to Archer River 116km.

Be cautious of livestock on the Batavia to Weipa Road

History of the Weipa district

The Aboriginal people have inhabited Australia for at least 40,000 years. The Cape York Aborigines practised traditional hunting well into the 1900's. In the late 1800's the Aboriginal people of the Weipa district had increased contact with Europeans due to the commencement of béche-de-mer fishing, pearling and the establishment of pastoral areas. Aborigines were recruited to assist with fishing, but due to misunderstandings on both sides the Presbyterian Church established a series of missionary stations to protect them. The first of these stations was opened up in November 1891 at Mapoon and soon missions were opened up in Weipa and Aurukun. Because of problems with the soil, water supplies and termites the Weipa mission station was moved to Jessica Point, now Napranum, in 1932.

There were numerous small Aboriginal settlements scattered through the area and these tribal groups far outnumbered the white settlers in the Weipa district. There were no significant changes in this area until 1955 when Harry Evans, a geologist, discovered bauxite, the raw material for aluminium. Following this discovery Comalco then established the mining township of Weipa in 1962. Over the years Comalco has expanded its operation and today Weipa has a population of approximately 3,500 and the mining and Aboriginal community live side by side.

Weipa

The township of Weipa was developed by Comalco for its mining personnel. Comalco was responsible for providing housing, electricity, a water supply plus all the associated facilities such as schools, parks, roads for mine workers and their families. Because of Weipa's location all buildings are cyclone resistant.

Most of the town's facilities are located at Rocky Point and Trunding. At Nanum there are 2 shopping centres, one a Woolworths complex with butchers, a hot bread shop, and a variety of other stores. At Woolworths you can use your EFTPOS Card for supplies. The other complex has a 7 to 11 Convenience Store, newsagent and post office. Nearby is the Paxhaven Camping Ground and a sporting complex. There are a number of sporting clubs and visitors are welcome. You can have a round at the local golf club and meals are available. Enquiries and bookings on: 0740 69-7300. The local library has an interesting display on Cape York.

Another popular spot is the bowls club, which also offers dining. Bookings on: 0740 69-7300. There are also a Lions Club and a Masonic Lodge. The Albatross Hotel-Motel at Trunding Point is airconditioned and has accommodation, counter meals and of course a cold beer, and there is a drive-in-bottle shop. Ph: 0740 69-7314 for enquiries. There is a cinema, and pick up a copy of the "Bauxite Bulletin" to see what's on, plus other information on facilities. Campbells Coaches operate daily town and mine tours. Enquiries and bookings on: 0740 69-7871.

For mechanical assistance:

Weipa Service Centre
Boundary Road,
Ph: 0740 69-7277
(Also RACQ Breakdown Service)
A/H 0740 69-9280

Wraftec Industries
1 Iraci Avenue,
Ph: 0740 69-7877
Fax: 0740 69-7909

WEIPA

AND

"THE CAPE"

Produced by
The Weipa Tourism and Development Association

THE WEIPA TOURISM AND DEVELOPMENT ASSOCIATION 1991

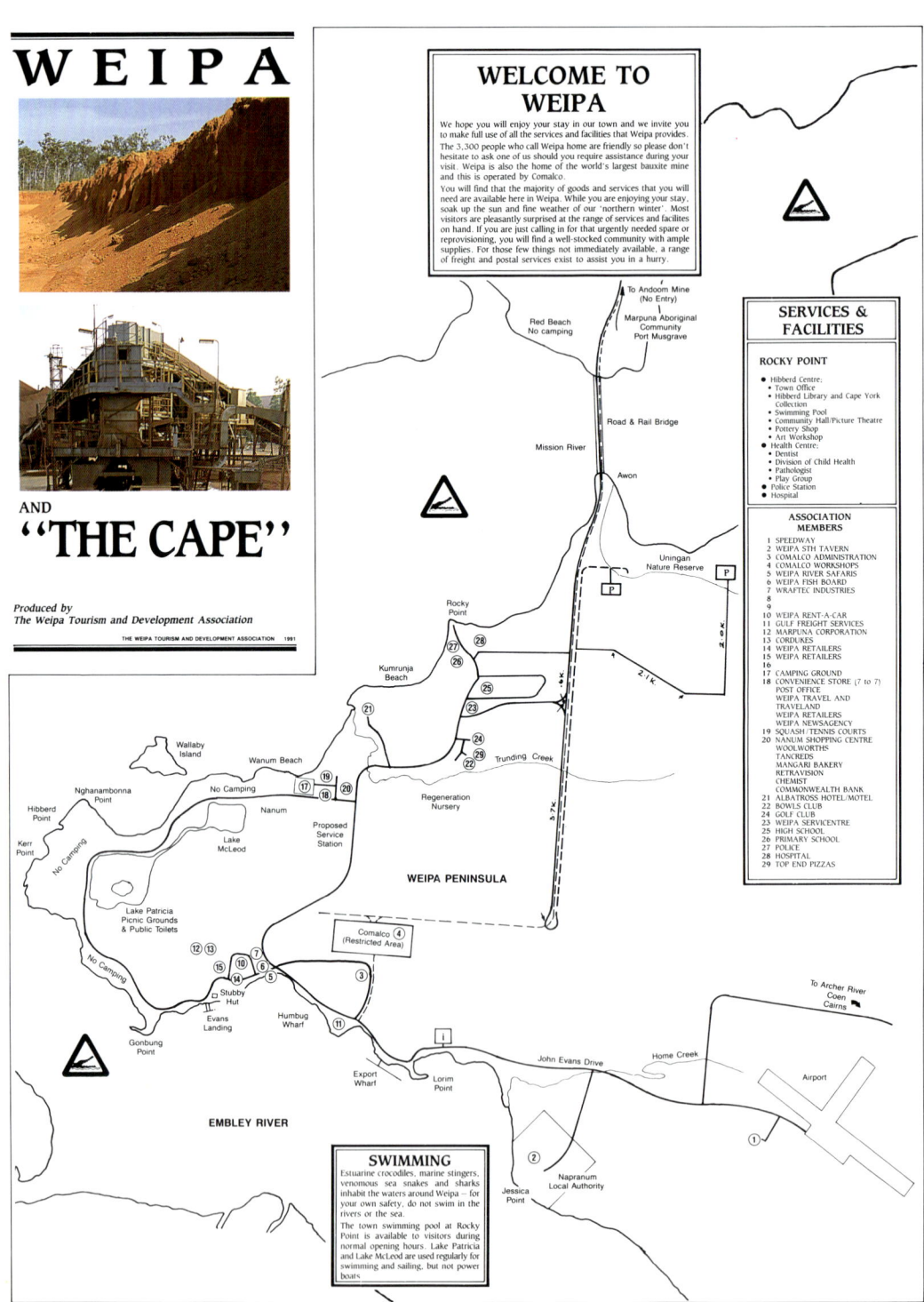

WELCOME TO WEIPA

We hope you will enjoy your stay in our town and we invite you to make full use of all the services and facilities that Weipa provides.

The 3,300 people who call Weipa home are friendly so please don't hesitate to ask one of us should you require assistance during your visit. Weipa is also the home of the world's largest bauxite mine and this is operated by Comalco.

You will find that the majority of goods and services that you will need are available here in Weipa. While you are enjoying your stay, soak up the sun and fine weather of our 'northern winter'. Most visitors are pleasantly surprised at the range of services and facilites on hand. If you are just calling in for that urgently needed spare or reprovisioning, you will find a well-stocked community with ample supplies. For those few things not immediately available, a range of freight and postal services exist to assist you in a hurry.

SERVICES & FACILITIES

ROCKY POINT

- Hibberd Centre;
  - Town Office
  - Hibberd Library and Cape York Collection
  - Swimming Pool
  - Community Hall/Picture Theatre
  - Pottery Shop
  - Art Workshop
- Health Centre;
  - Dentist
  - Division of Child Health
  - Pathologist
  - Play Group
- Police Station
- Hospital

ASSOCIATION MEMBERS

1 SPEEDWAY
2 WEIPA STH TAVERN
3 COMALCO ADMINISTRATION
4 COMALCO WORKSHOPS
5 WEIPA RIVER SAFARIS
6 WEIPA FISH BOARD
7 WRAFTEC INDUSTRIES
8
10 WEIPA RENT-A-CAR
11 GULF FREIGHT SERVICES
12 MARPUNA CORPORATION
13 CORDURES
14 WEIPA RETAILERS
15 WEIPA RETAILERS
16
17 CAMPING GROUND
18 CONVENIENCE STORE (7 to 7)
  POST OFFICE
  WEIPA TRAVEL AND TRAVELAND
  WEIPA RETAILERS
  WEIPA NEWSAGENCY
19 SQUASH/TENNIS COURTS
20 NANUM SHOPPING CENTRE
  WOOLWORTHS
  TANCREDS
  MANGARI BAKERY
  RETRAVISION
  CHEMIST
  COMMONWEALTH BANK
21 ALBATROSS HOTEL/MOTEL
22 BOWLS CLUB
24 GOLF CLUB
23 WEIPA SERVICENTRE
25 HIGH SCHOOL
26 PRIMARY SCHOOL
27 POLICE
28 HOSPITAL
29 TOP END PIZZAS

To Andoom Mine (No Entry)

Marpuna Aboriginal Community Port Musgrave

Red Beach No camping

Road & Rail Bridge

Mission River

Awon

Uningan Nature Reserve

Rocky Point

Kumrunja Beach

Wallaby Island

Wanum Beach

No Camping

Nghanambonna Point

Hibberd Point

Nanum

Kerr Point

No Camping

Lake McLeod

Proposed Service Station

Regeneration Nursery

Trunding Creek

WEIPA PENINSULA

Lake Patricia Picnic Grounds & Public Toilets

No Camping

Stubby Hut

Evans Landing

Humbug Wharf

Gonbung Point

Comalco (Restricted Area)

To Archer River
Coen
Cairns

Export Wharf

Lorim Point

John Evans Drive

Home Creek

Airport

EMBLEY RIVER

Napranum Local Authority

Jessica Point

SWIMMING

Estuarine crocodiles, marine stingers, venomous sea snakes and sharks inhabit the waters around Weipa — for your own safety, do not swim in the rivers or the sea.

The town swimming pool at Rocky Point is available to visitors during normal opening hours. Lake Patricia and Lake McLeod are used regularly for swimming and sailing, but not power boats.

Reproduced with the kind permission of The Weipa Chamber of Commerce

Weipa Rent-A-Car Ph: 0740 69-7311 (At Airport). Weipa Smash Repairs, Evans Landing Ph: 0740 69-7933. For fuel and mechanical repairs Mobil Service Station Boundary Road Ph: 0740 69-7277 – Bankcard & EFTPOS Card. With daily flights from Cairns to Weipa most parts can be obtained in 24 hours from Cairns if they are in stock. Weipa Motors & Marine Outboards cater for motor bikes and outboard repairs. Weipa Taxi: 0740 69-7540.

Barges
Vehicles and passengers can be barged from Weipa to Karumba, contact:
Gulf Freight Services
Yapar Street
Karumba 4891
Ph: 0747 45-9333. Weipa Office. 0740 69-8619.

Transport from Cairns
There are regular flights to Weipa but with deregulation of the airline system operators may increase. At present there is a daily flight with Ansett Airline. Charter flights from Cairns can be organised by Wingz North Ph: 0740 35-9032. Local scenic flights are available with Weipa Air Charter Ph: 0740 69-7807.

Coach Services
Coral Coaches run a weekly service from Cairns:
Bookings and enquiries:
Ph: 0740 98-2600
Fax: 0740 98-1064

Emergency Numbers
Police	0740 69-9119
Doctor	0740 69-7297
Hospital	0740 69-9155
Ambulance	0740 69-7444

Department of Environment
Northern Cape York
District Office.
Memorial Square,
Central Avenue.
Weipa.
Ph: 0740 69-7908.
Fax: 0740 69-7739.

Native Kapok – Cochlospermum gillivraei

Silk Cotton Tree – Bombax ceiba

Paxhaven Campsite

Camping facilities at Weipa are excellent. Paxhaven is the only campsite in Weipa with no other camping allowed within a 15km radius of the town.

Paxhaven is owned by Campbell Coaches and managed by Ian and Gail Prewett. Its location next to Nanum Beach is enhanced by lush green lawns and shady trees and really is a haven after the dusty roads.

The facilities Ian and Gail offer are first class. There is a large amenities block including facilities for the disabled and a well-equipped laundry. Campsites are spacious and you can choose between powered and unpowered sites. B.B.Q. areas are provided throughout the park and fires are confined to these areas. For those lucky enough to catch that "Big One" a fish-cleaning bay is provided and you are requested to confine all fish cleaning to this area. Adjacent is a car wash area, and the telephones are located next to the office. Within walking distance are two shopping complexes, one with a Woolworths store, the other with a convenience store, newsagent, post office and close by is a sporting complex.

There are a number of tours to be taken in the area, but no visit to Weipa would be complete without a tour of the town and the Comalco Mine. Bookings and departures are only from the campsite. Ian conducts tours daily. His informative commentary will introduce you to the fascinating world of bauxite mining, so visit the office for details on this tour and all other information you require on fishing, places to visit, souvenirs and maps, ice, fishing safaris, boat and trailer hire, air charters and much more.

Paxhaven Camping Ground — Weipa

*Setting Sun over the Western Horizon
from Paxhaven Camping Ground*

There is also accommodation at Evans Landing. The Weipa Riverview Cabins offer comfortable accommodation on the banks of the Embley River. The cabins are simple but sufficient, all linen is supplied and some are air-conditioned, to suit all budgets. The cabins are twin share with tea-making facilities, T.V. & fridges. You can also tie up your boat on your doorstep. For all bookings Ph: 0740 69-9159. Fax: 0740 69-7259 or Paxhaven Campground.

The Weipa district has a lot to offer and we strongly suggest staying a couple of days, allowing plenty of time for a mine tour and exploration of the area.

The campsite offers excellent relaxation. It's is tranquil, and at the end of the day the dusty roads are forgotten as you sit back and watch the setting sun over the western horizon. To locate Nanum Beach and the campsite, follow the signs into Weipa and refer to our map if necessary. For information and bookings contact:

Ian and Gail Prewett
P.O. Box 197
Weipa 4874 Qld.
Ph: 0740 69-7871. A/H: 0740 69-7643
Fax: 0740 69-8211
No credit cards accepted

Travelling around Weipa

The Weipa Chamber of Commerce has produced a map of Cape York including Weipa. The proceeds from this map will go into the development and management of Cape York, the map can be purchased from the service station, newsagent, Paxhaven camping ground and through other outlets on the Cape.

It is an excellent map for finding your way around. Visitors to the area are requested to familiarize themselves with the Haul Road Crossings, these huge trucks cannot stop quickly so if you see one approaching stop at the crossing and wait for it to pass. **DO NOT DRIVE ON THE HAUL ROADS.** When exploring Weipa obey all signs so as not to interfere with any mining operations. Fishing is excellent in this area and a day out on the water would make a great change from the dusty roads.

WARNING: Estuarine Crocodiles inhabit this area, exercise caution especially when fishing. Swimming is not recommended, use the local pool. Well worth a visit is the Uningan Nature Reserve, the reserve is adjacent to the South bank of the Mission River from Awonga Point and extends Eastward to Pappan Creek. Walking tracks, foot bridges and mangrove walkways have been provided by volunteers to give access through the Western edge of the reserve. To fully appreciate the flora and fauna it is recommended that you take a tour with a Ranger – contact Napranum Council on: (070) 69 7855 for details. This area is a must for birdwatchers, naturalists or anyone who really appreciates nature.

12km South of the Weipa township is the Aboriginal & Islander community of Napranum established in 1932. About eight percent of the Comalco workforce are aborigines and islanders and many of them live at Napranum, the company operates a civil earthworks scheme and provides employment and training in earthmoving equipment.

Located between Nanum and Evans Landing is Lake Patricia and Lake McLeod, they make an ideal picnic spot and a great spot to relax and have a swim.

Discovering Weipa will enhance anyone's visit to the Cape as it has something for everyone and it is recommended you include a visit in your itinerary.

Comalco Mine

Geologist Harry Evans was searching for oil on Cape York in 1955 when he discovered large deposits of Bauxite in the Weipa area. The bauxite consists of the alumina bearing minerals of Gibbsite and Boehmite intermixed with Kaolin and Iron Oxides, Silica and small quantities of various heavy minerals. The Bauxite ore is in the form of small reddish pebbles or Pisolites varying in diameter from less than 1mm to 25mm, from this Bauxite metal Aluminium is made. In the early 60's Comalco was established to develop this resource and hence the development of Weipa and the mine. There are 3 steps involved in producing Aluminium, mining the Bauxite, refining the ore to alumina and then converting the Alumina to Aluminium metal. In order to meet customers requirements of correct blends sample drilling is undertaken, samples are analysed and the results are used to prepare a mining plan, this plan specifies which areas are to be mined and when. Bulldozers then clear the surface of the selected areas and the vegetation is piled up and burnt, scrapers then remove the top soil in depths from half to one metre, this soil is then transported as soon as possible to areas awaiting regeneration, to minimise damage occurring to seeds and nutrients etc. The Bauxite is then mined by huge rubber-tyred front-end loaders, and then loaded on to bottom-dump trailers of 150-tonne capacity. They then haul the bauxite from the mine pits to elevated dump stations located at Lorim Point (for Weipa Peninsula ore) and at Andoom (19km North of Lorim Point). Ore transport between Andoom and Lorim Point is by railway. The ore wagons have a capacity of 100 tonnes. Train loading and dumping stations are designed to operate on a continuous basis. The trains travel up to 80kph and complete the journey in about one hour. After the crude ore is unloaded at Lorim Point it is either stockpiled or fed directly into an ore distribution bin where the bauxite is sized and washed. It is then transported from stockpiles by means of gravity chutes feeding underground conveyors that are linked to one of the two shiploaders. Bauxite samples are taken while the ore is being stockpiled to ensure the correct grade is being supplied.

Most of the bauxite mined at Weipa is shipped to Gladstone in Central Queensland where it is refined into alumina. The remainder is exported to Japan, Europe, USA and USSR. It takes about four tonnes of Weipa bauxite to make two tonnes of alumina, which in turn yields one tonne of Aluminium.

Kaolin is also being mined at Weipa, in the areas selected where the bauxite has already been mined. After the kaolin has been processed it is stored in sealed silos and loaded on to ships by enclosed conveyors and ship loader. The Weipa kaolin ore is suitable for the production of high-quality paper coating clay.

At present, operations at the kaolin plant have ceased, but you can still view the silos.

Kaolin Silos at Weipa

Overleaf: Removing top soil from Comalco's Bauxite Mine

The massive machinery used in mining Bauxite

A mine tour takes you right amongst the machinery

Stockpiled Bauxite ready for shipping

Bauxite being transported between Andoom and Lorim Point by rail

All Bauxite leaving Weipa is transported by sea

After mining, sites are regenerated

Regeneration of mined areas

Comalco's lease agreement with the Queensland Government requires it to regenerate mined land, mining in Weipa is a simple open cut process. During actual mining clearing of native forest is kept to minimum and corridors are left to protect fauna. When regenerating an area fresh top soil is first spread containing organic matter and native seeds to a depth of 0.5 metre. Bulldozers then cut through the soil to a depth of 2 metres to assist drainage and root penetration.

Seeds are locally collected from native species and mixed with fertiliser and in the majority of areas spread by aircraft. Native trees and shrubs are grown in Comalco's nursery and are hand planted which helps establish species which are difficult to grow by aerial sowing. Native flora is planted so that ·fauna will return to regenerated areas and restore the ecological balance.

Taking a tour of the mine and regenerated areas will further explain all the steps involved in mining the Bauxite and restoration of these areas,it is thoroughly recommended.

Old Mapoon

If you wish to visit the Aboriginal Settlement of Mapoon, please contact:
The Chairperson
Weipa South and Mapoon Aboriginal Community
Weipa South Qld 4874
Ph: 0740 69-7855

Weipa – Stones Crossing – 69km

Heading towards Andoom, Stones Crossing is signposted. Turn right at the Mapoon sign and follow the track. You may experience some directional difficulties here due to the mass of seismic tracks. All we can suggest is to follow the signs and keep to the main track. You cross Woodford Lagoon just before Stones Crossing.

Stones Crossing

Situated on the mighty Wenlock, this area is perfect for camping. There are many ideal sites along the banks, the fishing is good and this spot is very popular with the locals. We spotted a crocodile while we were there, so swimming is not recommended. There are, however, some shallow rapids at the crossing itself, but keep an eye out. The road North from Stones Crossing passes through Bertihaugh Station and is a private road.

Stones Crossing

128

Iron Range National Park

Iron Range National Park covers approximately 34,600 hectares plus a further 20,000 hectares of Department and Official Purpose Reserves. These Department and Official Purpose Reserves are special purpose reserves used for natural resource protection.

Both National Parks and Department and Official Purpose Reserves come under the jurisdiction of the National Parks and are managed and controlled by an on-sight Ranger located within the park itself.

Firstly on entering Iron Range National Park call at the Rangers Station located along the Lockhart River road there you can be advised on the tourist and camping facilities within the park. Depending on climatic conditions certain roads and campsites may be closed for the benefit of the public's safety or to allow certain areas to regenerate so as to keep the park in its most pristine condition.

National Parks and Wildlife Service permits are required for camping in Iron Range campsites, Chili Beach, Claudie and Gordon Creek. These permits must be obtained before setting up camp and camping in this area is bush style so make sure you have a full complement of provisions and water. If the Ranger is not in attendance refer to the information board at the Rangers Station then proceed to your camping spot, the Ranger will see you there, but please go to the station first.

As you enter the park through the Western edge you pass the rugged hills of Janet and Tozer Ranges with their sheer cliffs, a spectacular sight with the early morning sun glistening upon them. Mt Tozer is 543m above sea level making it the highest mountain in the region.

The vegetation varies dramatically in this park from open woodlands, dense rainforests to paper bark forests right down to mangrove fringed coastal vegetation.

Entrance to Iron Range National Park

The National Park itself is of world significance as it conserves the largest area of lowland rainforest in Australia. The rainforest supports a wide range of wildlife and birdlife from Palm Cockatoos to Cassowaries and Green Pythons to the Spotted Cuscus. The rainforest makes a welcome and cool change from the drier and much hotter interior of Cape York Peninsula.

The Southern and Western boundaries of the park are bordered by Aboriginal lands. Apart from the main road any entry into Aboriginal land requires approval from the local Aboriginal Council – in this case Lockhart River Community Council. Ph: 0740 60-7144 or call in at the council and have a talk with the Aboriginal Ranger on duty.

Aborigines from the Kuuku Yau Tribe lived scattered throughout the area until the mid 1920's then they were relocated to Missions, firstly at Orchid Point then Old Site. Now their descendants live at the Lockhart River Community Mission and still retain their close ties with their heritage.

Iron Range National Park offers the visitor diverse activities, as it is an ideal location for special interest groups, keen birdwatchers and all lovers of nature. The variety of flora and fauna, some of which are found in no other region of Australia, will impress any visitor.

Please help to preserve the Iron Range National Park by observing the following:

- Leave all plant material, native and other components undisturbed. Remember this area is totally protected.
- Leave pets outside the park.
- Use vehicles only on main roads and tracks.
- Take care with fire. Preferably use a fuel stove.
- Do not use soap or detergent in any streams, rivers or waterholes.
- Take your rubbish with you. Properly burnt and crushed, rubbish is easy to transport and odourless.
- Fishing is prohibited.
- Firearms are prohibited.
- Be considerate of others.

For further information, contact:
The Ranger,
Iron Range National Park,
Lockhart River Qld 4871
0740 60-7170

Golden Bouquet – Deplanchea tetraphylla

WEYMOUTH BAY

RIVER

PASCOE

JANET

CONSERVATION
AND
MINING RESERVES

PORTLAND
ROADS

7

CHILI
BEACH

IRON RANGE
NATIONAL PARK

6.5

RANGE

19.5

CAPE
GRIFFITH

27

FRENCHMANS
ROAD

3

CONSERVATION

MT. TOZER

3.5

98 TO ARCHER RIVER

TOZER

RANGER
STATION

8

LOCKHART

RIVER
ABORIGINAL
COMMUNITY

RESERVE

AIRPORT

RANGE

LLOYD
BAY

PASCOE

RIVER

MAP NOT TO SCALE

131

Archer River To Portland Roads – Lockhart River – 🏠 📷 ✂ ✚
Iron Range – 🏠 Chili Beach 🏠

Approximately 20km North of Archer River, turn right for Portland Roads, Lockhart River and Iron Range National Park. Drive 26km to the Wenlock River. There is a nice camping spot on the left on the river bed if the river is not too high. Across the river to the left is a track leading to the Old Wenlock shed and you can camp here also if you wish. 32km further on brings you to the Pascoe River. This really is a good camping spot and an ideal stopover. 20km further a track joins from the left, which is known as Frenchmans Road and can be travelled on the return journey from Iron Range. Frenchmans Road meets up with the Telegraph Track 98km North of the Archer River (Frenchmans Road detailed track note page 135).

From the Frenchmans Road intersection to the Iron Range, Portland Roads turnoff is 27km. Along this section of road you cross several small creeks flowing into the Pascoe River. These crossings are ideal picnic stopovers as the Gallery Forests line the banks making them superb wildlife corridors.

You are now entering Iron Range National Park so please obey National Park rules. The Ranger's Station is at Kings Park Homestead and located on the Lockhart River Road 3.5km from the Portland Roads turnoff, just before the Lockhart River Airfield. You require a permit to camp in Iron Range and at Chili Beach. No camping is allowed at Portland Roads. You can organise your permit at the Ranger's Station and all relevant information on the area. The Ranger can also advise you of the best camping spots and anything of particular interest in his area.

When camping where there are no facilities remember to dig holes to bury human waste and take all rubbish with you.

8km past the Ranger Station on the Lockhart River Road brings you to the Lockhart River Aboriginal Community, where you are welcome to get supplies. There is a well-stocked store and fuel is available, but only Mon-Fri. There is some mechanical assistance, but it may be limited, there are telephones and a Post Office. A weekly barge calls here and there is a daily flight from Cairns – for schedules, phone the Lockhart River Community Office on: 0740 60-7144 for any details on this area. Police 0740 60-7120. Hospital 0740 60-7155.

You are asked to respect the community's privacy and not use cameras or videos in the town. You are welcome to take photos etc. anywhere on the beach. (The road to the Old Lockhart River Mission is definitely closed to all traffic.)

Wenlock Crossing on Lockhart River Road

Pascoe River on Lockhart River Road

Iron Range Ranger Station to Portland Roads — 33km

At approximately 26km from the Ranger Station is the right hand turn to Chili Beach. It is sign posted just before the track, straight ahead 7km brings you into the Roads. It is a very sleepy hamlet with spectacular scenery, most properties in the area are privately owned. The bay is used by yachts and trawlers for shelter, the trawlers also refuel here from a Dumb Barge which is towed up from Cairns. At low tide you can explore around the rocks, but don't walk on the reef. The marine life is very interesting, fishing is excellent either from the rocks or a boat.

WARNING: Swimming or snorkelling is not recommended due to Estuarine Crocodiles inhabiting the area.

There are limited facilities here, toilets are available and a public well. There is a small cafe, but it is only open seasonally, with limits on trading hours, Telecom have now installed 2 telephone boxes. Portland Roads is indeed a picturesque spot and we recommend the visit. If intending to camp at Chili Beach, replenish your water here (there is no drinking water at Chili Beach).

Aerial view of Portland Roads as seen on your Wingz North Scenic Flight

Even in rough weather Chili Beach is still beautiful

Chili Beach – Carry drinking water

The 6.5km track into the beach is gravel and causes no real problems. The camping area is under National Parks control so a permit is required. Camping spots are spread out along the beach set back towards the vegetation. This area is subject to very strong winds so find the best sheltered spot. There are a number of bores but the water is suitable for washing only.

Chili Beach is an ideal camping spot. Its coconut-fringed beach makes it very tropical, and the only disadvantage is the strong winds experienced along the coast during the dry season.

As Iron Range National Park is in a higher rainfall bracket than the rest of the Cape, rainfall can cause the visitor to panic. A mass exodus from the area during rain only causes the road to become impassable and dangerous to travel. The Ranger's recommendation is to stay put for the day, allowing the road to dry out again and be safe to traverse. If you have done the right thing on entering the park and procured your camping permit the Ranger knows where to find you in case of climatic changes.

Iron Range Ranger Station to Telegraph Track via Frenchmans Road — 83kms

Approximately 30km from the Iron Range Ranger Station you will on your right find the Frenchmans Road turnoff. Travelling this most scenic road on the Cape at the llkm point you cross the Pascoe River, down through a steep canyon, across the Pascoe River, up and out of the canyon on the other side (no available camping here). From the Pascoe River another 29km brings you to the Wenlock River with good water and good camping in the gravel along the river bed. From the Wenlock River to the Telegraph Track is only another 13km. When reaching the Telegraph Track, turn right (North) 20km to the Telegraph Track Road, Wenlock River crossing (good camping but can be a little cramped during the height of the season). Turning left (South) will take you back to the Archer River 98km or travel only 2km from the turnoff and on your right you will see the Batavia Downs Airstrip. Turn right down alongside the Airstrip and follow this road to Weipa.

WARNING: Crocodiles are present in the creeks, rivers and waterholes and along the beaches of Cape York. Do not swim or prepare food at water's edge or camp within 50m of deep water where these animals may be present.

Frenchmans Road looking back to Iron Range where the highest rainfall occurs on the Cape

Pascoe River Crossing – Frenchmans Road

Good camping amongst the Melaleuca's on the Wenlock River on Frenchmans Road

Mungkan Kaanju National Park. (Formerly Rokeby) 🏠

The National Park is one of five large Peninsula Parks in Central Cape York. Together with Archer Bend National Park it covers 457,000 hectares from the West foothills of the McIlwraith Ranges and to the West of the junction of the Archer and Coen Rivers. These rivers are major features of the park. Dense rainforests cover the heights of the McIlwraith Ranges at the Eastern end of the park. Further West the rainforest reduces to narrow bands along the rivers. These narrow bands of rainforest provide wildlife corridors allowing animals to move from one area to another.

Much of the area is covered by dry, open woodland of Eucalypts, with seasonally wet Melaleuca, also known as Paperbarks, occupying much of the area between the Archer and Coen Rivers. The park is an ideal location for those wishing to really get away from civilisation and have an intimate contact with nature. It is perfect for birdwatchers with a wide variety of species, and walks around lagoons and swamps will delight visitors. When walking along rivers and waterholes you may sight crocodiles, Palm Cockatoos and other wildlife. The whole area is perfect for serious hikers.

Access to the park is through Coen to the Rokeby access road turnoff 22km North of Coen and then West to Rokeby Ranger Base 66 km, which will take you approximately 2 hours. Roads into the park are suitable only for 4WD vehicles. Because of the remoteness of the park all visitors are requested to check in at the Ranger's Base, this is for your safety. Although there are no developed camping grounds, bush camping is permitted at a number of sites adjacent to rivers and waterholes, but a permit is required and can be obtained from the Ranger Base. At the base you can obtain a visitor's information sheet and any other information on the area including the historical aspects of Mungkan Kaanju National Park.

During your visit you must be totally self-sufficient. Make sure your vehicle is in good mechanical condition, as no fuel or spare parts or mechanical assistance is available, and carry water as there are long stretches along the roads where no water is available.

In order to protect the park you are requested to observe the following:
• Take your rubbish with you or take it to the base for disposal.
• Bury all human waste.
• Take extreme care with fire.
• Keep to formed roads and tracks.
• Do not bring domestic pets or firearms into the park.
• Fishing is prohibited throughout the park.
• Do not use soap or detergents in any stream, river or waterhole.

WARNING: Estuarine Crocodiles are present in freshwater holes and rivers. These animals are potentially dangerous, so stay away from deep water. Do not prepare food by the water's edge. Report any sightings of large crocodiles to the Ranger. Freshwater Crocodiles, identified by their narrow jaw, also inhabit the park, and feed on insects and fish, but will attack humans if threatened. Familiarize yourself with the two species.

For further information contact:
The Ranger
Mungkan Kaanju National Park
P.M.B. 28, Cairns Mail Centre
Qld 4870
Ph: 0740 60-3256.

Mungkan Kaanju and Archer Bend N.P. were formerly operated as cattle stations under a grazing lease. The Rokeby Ranger Base site was the centre of management for these cattle operations.

With the declaration of Archer Bend National Park in 1979 and Rokeby National Park in 1982, both parks were subsequently destocked by the Queensland Department of Primary Industries, the Queensland National Parks and Wildlife Service and the former owners of the cattle property. Rokeby has now been renamed Mungkan Kaanju National Park.

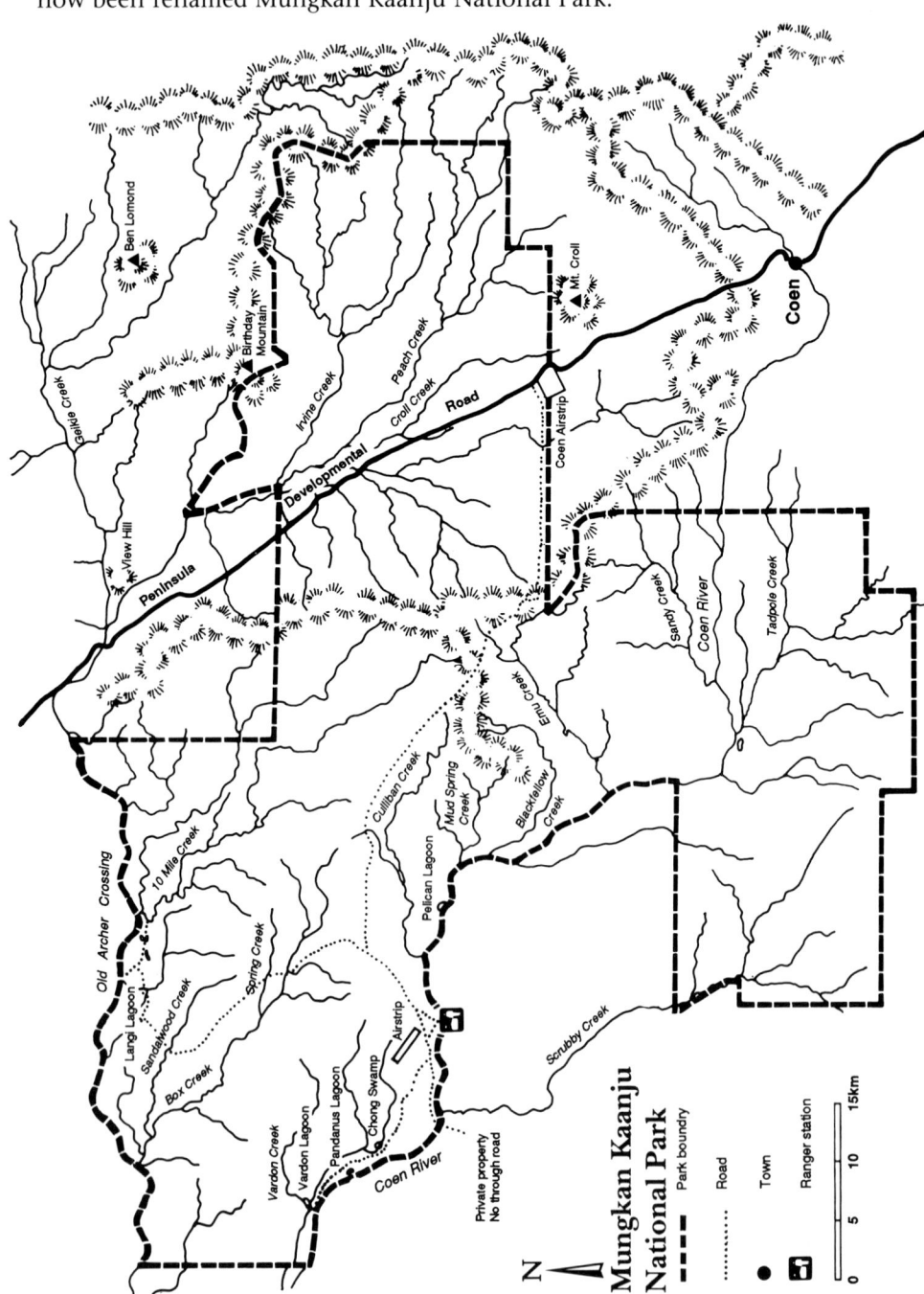

Coen – Port Stewart — 90kms

Travelling South from Coen 27km you will find on your left the turnoff to Port Stewart. After following this track along through the high country you descend down onto the lower plains country. At the 34km mark the road forks, the righthand track continues on to Port Stewart another 29km with the lefthand track leading to Silver Plains Cattle Station (Private Property).

Port Stewart – No freshwater

Port Stewart is an ideal fishing and crabbing spot. There is an area to launch your boat and you can either fish the Stewart River or the coast from the river's mouth.

Camping is bush style with no facilities available, there is no fresh drinking water so carry an ample supply. Estuarine Crocodiles do inhabit this area so swimming is not recommended, we also found the mosquitoes a big problem on dusk, but only for half an hour, so carry plenty of repellent.

Mouth of the Stewart River

Good fishing and crabbing in the Stewart River

Remains of the Old Silver Plains Homestead alongside the Port Stewart road

Lakefield National Park 🏕

Lakefield has an area of 537,000 hectares, making it Queensland's second-largest National Park and the most accessible on Cape York. The park has extensive river systems, including the Normanby, Morehead and North Kennedy Rivers. During the wet season these rivers join other water courses and flood the region, eventually draining into Princess Charlotte Bay. The rivers, lagoons and swamps provide a habitat for great varieties of birds and wildlife. Most of the park is covered by grasslands and woodlands. To the North mudflats and mangroves line the coast and the estuary systems of the Normanby and North Kennedy Rivers.

The abundance of wildlife in this park gives a unique opportunity for photography around the swamps and lagoons. Wild pigs forage regularly, and many a Brolga, Jabiru and Egret can be seen taking a leisurely feed. Two species of crocodiles are found in Lakefield. The Freshwater Crocodile, recognised by its narrow jaws, only inhabitat freshwater rivers and lagoons and is usually quite harmless if left alone. The Estuarine Crocodile, however, is potentially dangerous. It is easily identified by its broader jaws and inhabits salt and fresh waters. Lakefield is one of only six key areas for Estuarine Crocodile conservation in Queensland and is crucial to the long-term conservation of this species. Visitors to the park are asked to respect this important role in the State's crocodile management program and report any sightings of large crocodiles to the Ranger.

The main access to Lakefield National Park is from Cairns via the Peninsula Development Road to Laura (approximately 315km) and then North to the New Laura Ranger Station. This is the only access for two-wheel-drive vehicles – with extreme care needed. The road can become impassable after rain. Ordinary vehicles can go on to Lakefield Homestead, Bizant and Hann Crossing with care. However, 4WD vehicles are always recommended. 4WD access from Cooktown is via Battle Camp Road and from Musgrave via Saltwater Creek. Bush camping is permitted at a number of sites along rivers and waterholes, but a permit is required from the rangers at Lakefield. There are three Ranger Stations:

New Laura – Ph: 0740 60-3260
Lakefield – Ph: 0740 60-3271
Bizant – Ph: 0740 60-3258

A visit to these stations will enable you to obtain all information on visiting this area, and the rangers will be only too pleased to assist you in any way. You have to be self-sufficient while visiting the park as there are no supplies, fuel or mechanical assistance available. Make sure your vehicle is in good condition and carry spare parts and adequate provisions and water. In order to help protect the park you are requested to observe the following:

- Take all rubbish with you, do not bury it. Bury all human waste if toilets are not available, away from campsites and rivers and creeks.
- Keep to formed roads and tracks open to the public.
- Take extreme care with fire. The open forest and grasslands are very vulnerable to bushfires.
- Do not bring domestic animals or firearms into the park.
- Do not use soap or detergent in rivers, creeks and waterholes.

WARNING: Estuarine Crocodiles are present in freshwater holes and rivers. These animals are potentially dangerous. Stay away from deep water, do not prepare food by the water's edge, and erect your camp at least 50m from the water's edge.

A good way to explore the park is to camp at different locations. The Ranger can suggest a campsite that suits your vehicle and requirements.

For information and bookings contact:

The Rangers
Lakefield National Park
P.M.B. 29,
Cairns Mail Centre 4870
Ph: 0740 60-3271

The Ranger
Bizant
P.M.B. 30,
Cairns Mail Centre 4870
Ph: 0740 60-3258

The Ranger
New Laura P.M.B 79,
Cairns Mail Centre 4870
Ph: 0740 60-3260

Jabiru (Black-Neck-Stork)

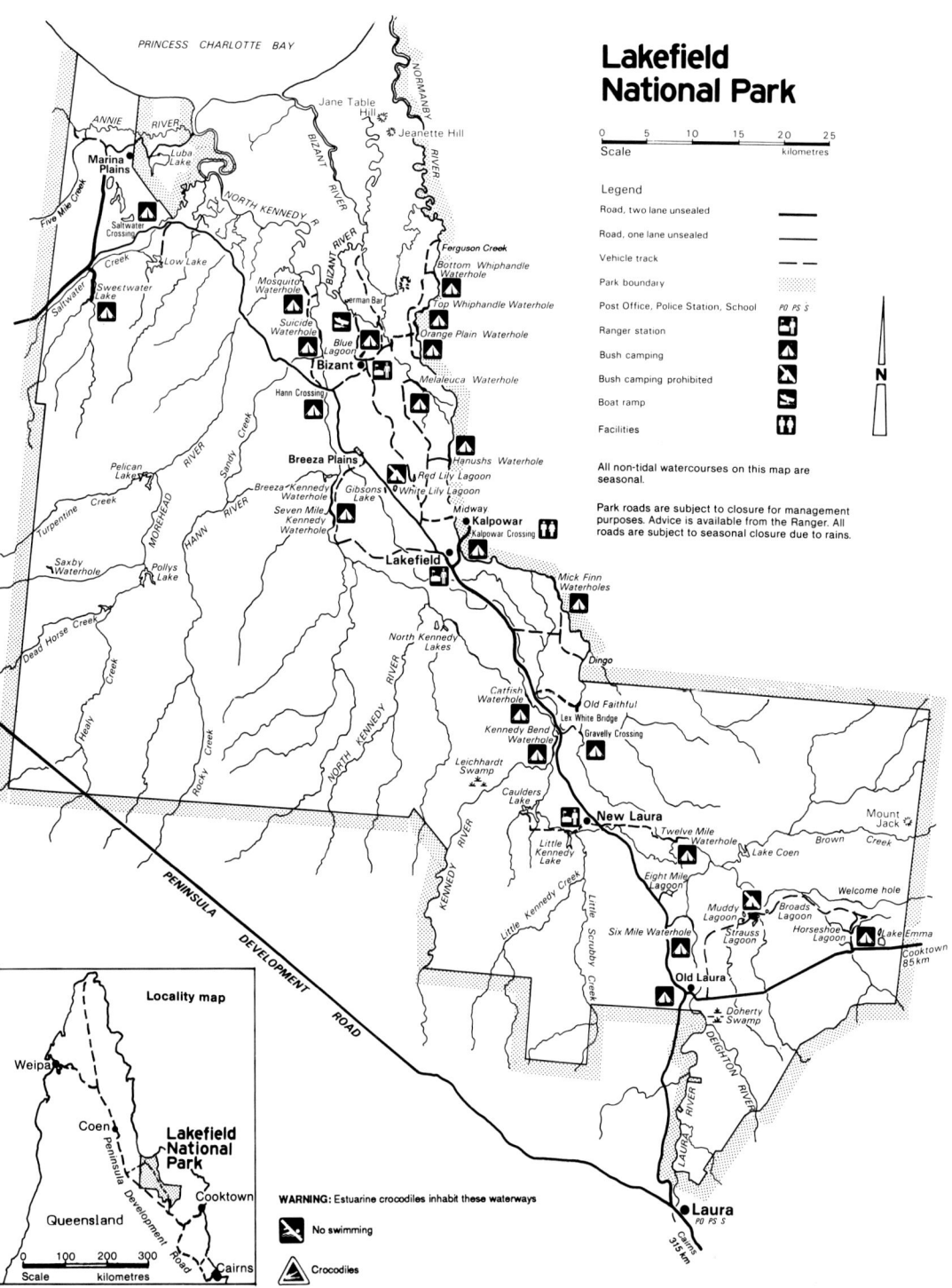

Lakefield National Park

Reproduced with the kind permission of the Department of Environment and Heritage

Living monuments to the silent termite

A birdwatchers' paradise around all of the lakes located in Lakefield National Park

Female Red-tailed Black Cockatoo

Estuarine Crocodile devouring a wallaby in Lakefield National Park

Goannas are found in abundance in Lakefield National Park

Take extreme care with fire, the open forest and grasslands are very vulnerable to bushfires

Cairns to Cooktown via Coast Road (235km)

The Cairns to Cooktown road is one of the most scenic roads in Australia to travel, passing alongside white sandy beaches fringed by the Great Barrier Reef, and traversing mountains that are heavily timbered with some of the most dense rainforests ever found in Australia.

Between the Daintree and Bloomfield Rivers is Cape Tribulation National Park where the rainforest and views are most spectacular. (For details on the National Park see page 148.)

The road from Cairns to the Daintree Ferry is bitumen and open to traffic all year round. The Daintree Ferry operates 7 days a week from 6am – midnight with a carrying capacity of 18 cars per trip. From the Daintree River Ferry to Cooktown is a dirt road. 2WD vehicles can access Cape Tribulation only during the dry season. Travelling North from Cape Tribulation is by 4WD only.

Further along this road you cross the Bloomfield River by the new causeway that has been built.

32km South of Cooktown is the Lions Den Hotel. This hotel was built around 1875 and still retains much of its character and history and is well worth a visit (fuel, meals, camping). Ph: 0740 60-3911. 4km North of the hotel you enter a T-intersection. Turning left here is the inland road back to Cairns via Lakeland, turning right takes you to Cooktown via Black Mountain National Park, which is steeped in Aboriginal myths and legends.

For a report on the road conditions from Cairns to Cooktown contact: The RACQ on Ph: 0740 33-6711 (24-hour Service Road Report).

The whole area from Cains to Cooktown is very popular with visitors. There are many accommodation outlets and tours too numerous to mention.

For further information contact:
The Far North Queensland Promotion Bureau
Cnr. Grafton & Hartley Streets,
Cairns 4870. Qld.
Ph: 0740 51-3588
Fax: 0740 51-0127

Mouth of the Daintree River

Cape Tribulation National Park 🏕️ 🏚️

The park extends along the coast between the Bloomfield and Daintree Rivers and inland to the McDowall Ranges, and covers 16,959 hectares. This is where the rainforest meets the sea with long stretches of sandy beaches and rocky headlands. The forests are home to varied fauna and a new species of rat has been discovered in the park, set in the lush tropics. Camping is permitted at Noah Beach, and toilets and water is provided. A permit is required and this can be obtained from the Ranger. There is a public camping ground at Thornton Beach and private camping area at Myall Creek.

At Cape Tribulation, named by Captain Cook, there is a private camping ground and a multitude of hostels and holiday units. There are many activities to be undertaken in this area. A boardwalk has been provided at the Cape Tribulation carpark leading to a viewing platform overlooking the ocean. At Oliver Creek, a 800m walking track provides a unique aspect of the rainforest and mangroves, and there are many beach walks to be taken along the coast. The beach, reef and coastal waters are under the protection of Marine Parks. Fishing, spearing or collecting is prohibited. South of Cape Tribulation limited fishing by line is permitted. Check a zoning map for the definitions.

While in this National and Marine Park you are asked to observe the following:

• Camp in designated areas.
• Please use fuel stoves for all cooking.
• Do not drive off formed roads.
• Do not bring pets into the park.
• Firearms, axes, machetes, chainsaws and generators are prohibited.

WARNING: Estuarine Crocodiles are present in most creeks and in the Daintree and Bloomfield Rivers. From October to April the presence of Marine Stingers makes swimming in the sea dangerous.

For further details contact:
Queensland National Parks and Wildlife Service
Cnr. Front & Johnston Streets
P.O. Box 251
Mossman
Qld. 4873.
Ph: 0740 98-2188

Bloomfield Track where the rainforest meets the sea

The old Bloomfield River crossing.

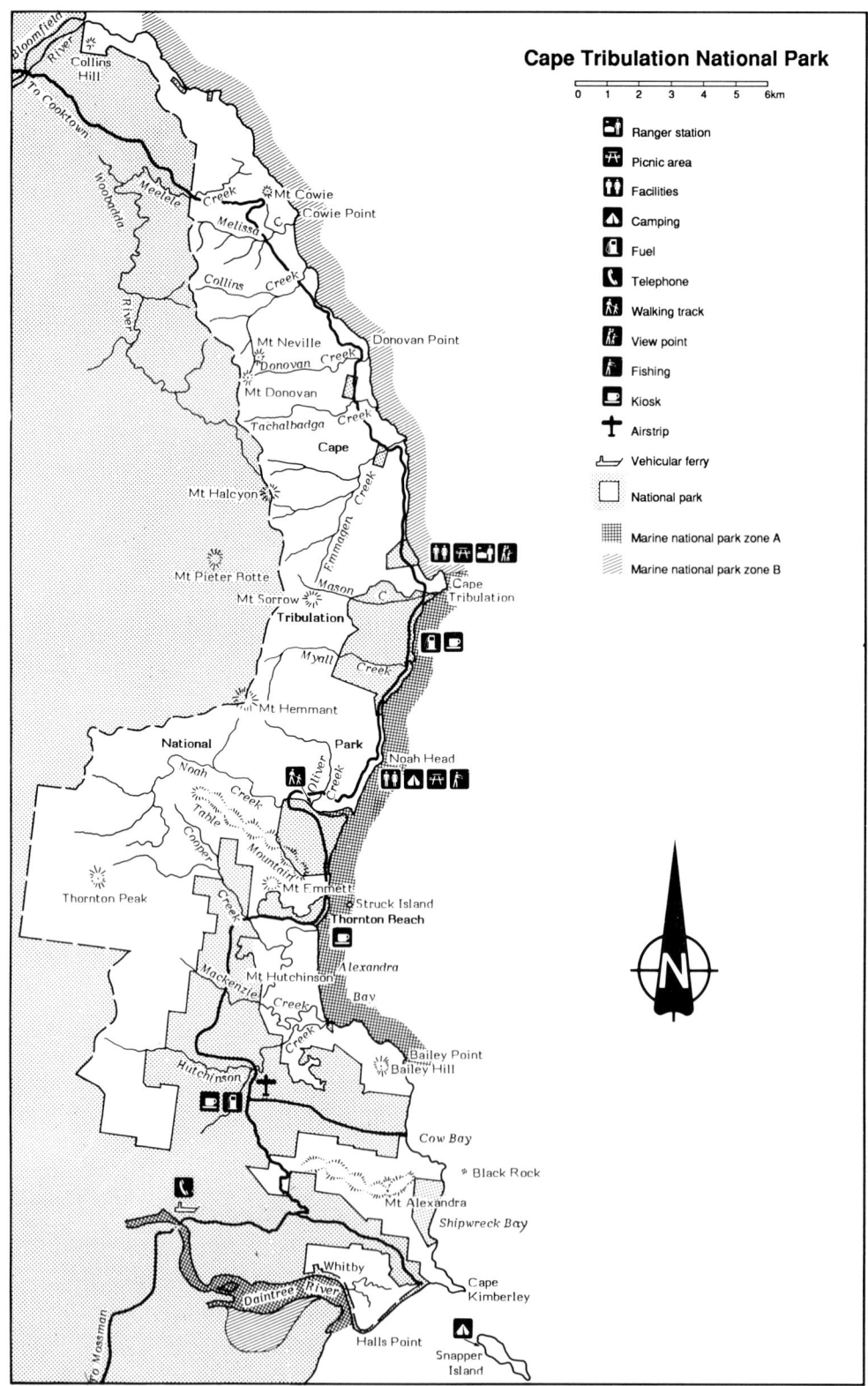

Cape Tribulation National Park

0 1 2 3 4 5 6km	

- Ranger station
- Picnic area
- Facilities
- Camping
- Fuel
- Telephone
- Walking track
- View point
- Fishing
- Kiosk
- Airstrip
- Vehicular ferry
- National park
- Marine national park zone A
- Marine national park zone B

Bloomfield River
Collins Hill
To Cooktown
Woobadda River
Meelele Creek
Melissa Creek
Mt Cowie
Cowie Point
Collins Creek
C.
Mt Neville
Donovan Creek
Donovan Point
Donovan
Mt Donovan
Tachalbadga Creek
Cape
Mt Halcyon
Emmagen Creek
Mt Pieter Botte
Mason C.
Mt Sorrow
Cape Tribulation
Tribulation
Myall Creek
Mt Hemmant
National
Noah Creek
Oliver Creek
Park
Noah Head
Table Mountain
Cooper Creek
Thornton Peak
Mt Emmett
Struck Island
Thornton Beach
Alexandra
Mackenzie Creek
Mt Hutchinson
Bay
Hutchinson Creek
Bailey Point
Bailey Hill
Cow Bay
Black Rock
Mt Alexandra
Shipwreck Bay
Whitby
Daintree River
Cape Kimberley
To Mossman
Halls Point
Snapper Island

N

Reproduced with the kind permission of the Department of Environment and Heritage

Strong Aboriginal legends surround Black Mountain, South of Cooktown

Old wooden bridge over the Annan River, South of Cooktown

Cooktown

Cooktown was named in 1770 after Captain James Cook, who beached his vessel the Endeavour on the Southern banks of the Endeavour River to undertake repairs after running aground on one of the many reefs that fringe this coastline.

For over another 100 years the area remained a peaceful, tranquil location inhabited only by Aborigines, but in 1873 all this came to an abrupt end when gold was discovered in the Palmer River by James Venture Mulligan. It was decided that the site of Cook's landing on the Endeavour River would be used as a base for the trek to the goldfields and would become a Far Northern seaport.

On October 25th 1873 the steam ship Leichhardt arrived with building materials, officials and prospectors to establish the township of 'Cooks Town'. Prospectors poured in from everywhere and the town grew quickly. The town boasted 65 hotels, 20 eating houses and 32 general stores. By 1885 Cooktown's population exceeded 35,000, including thousands of Chinese.

Cooktown depended on the mining of gold for its survival, and after the removal of tons of gold production began to decline. By the turn of the century the population was barely 2,000, but with the growing pearling and cattle industry the town managed to survive. During the Second World War most of the town was evacuated, and in 1949 a cyclone almost destroyed it. Cooktown survived and today it is one of the biggest tourist attractions in North Queensland.

Exploring Cooktown

It is well worth spending a few days in this historic town, which is steeped in history. The James Cook Historical Museum located on Helen and Furneaux Streets houses Cooktown's past, and a visit is a must to get a better understanding of what pioneers in those days endured. The Cooktown Sea Museum on Walker Street conducts tours through the museum, which houses many nautical relics. The Endeavour River Gallery is located in the Sovereign complex, Charlotte Street, and is well worth a visit. The historical Botanical Gardens on Walker Street have been upgraded by the Cook Shire Council and are a must for all visitors. You can access the beach from here by two walking tracks through the gardens.

The Cooktown Cemetery and Chinese Shrine located at the end of Charlotte Street is fascinating. The young age of many who have died reflects the harshness of the pioneering era.

For spectacular views of the surrounding district a trip to the lighthouse on Grassy Hill is a must. Take your camera – it is also an excellent spot to photograph sunsets over the Endeavour River. Along the foreshore fringing parklands surround Captain Cook's monument – a tribute to an early explorer's courage, this area is also ideal for picnics.

There are many scenic drives around the area. Finch and Walkers Bays are well worth a visit (4WD vehicles only). Cooktown caters very well for visitors. There are many tour operators in the area offering a wide selection of activities; there are cruises exploring the Endeavour River, fishing safaris and coach tours to surrounding areas. Full information is available from all accommodation outlets.

Overleaf: Sunset over the Endeavour River – Cooktown

Pioneering defence equipment of old Cooktown

Cooktown Jetty is a popular place for fishing

Cooktown's Facilities

The town has a number of general stores, including a newsagency, chemist and hardware. At the Cooktown Motor Inn and general store you can hire a number of 4WD vehicles. You can also use your EFTPOS card for groceries. There is a Westpac Bank on Charlotte Street and a Commonwealth Bank agency at the Post Office. For Cooktown Taxi Service contact: 0740 69-5387.

Fuel and Mechanical Assistance   Auto Gas Available

Ampol Driveway
Hope Street
Cooktown Qld. 4871   Your Ampol Card is
Ph: 0740 69-5354   welcome here

Cape York Tyres (RACQ Breakdown Service)
Charlotte Street
Cooktown Qld. 4871
Ph: 0740 69-5233
Full mechanical services, fuel, oils, gas refills, some parts. Accepted credit cards: Bankcard, Mastercard, Visa. EFTPOS facilities.

ACCOMMODATION AND CAMPING

Caravan/Camping

Cooktown Tropical Breeze	Junction Charlotte St. & McIvor Rd. Ph: 0740 69-5417.
Endeavour Falls Tourist Park	McIvor Rd. Ph: 0740 69-5431.
Golden Orchid C/Park	Charlotte St. Ph: 0740 69-5641.
Peninsula C/Park	Howard St. Ph: 0740 69-5107.

Motel/Hotel

Alamanda Inn	Hope St. Ph: 0740 69-5203.
Cooktown Hotel	Cnr Charlotte St. & Walker St. Ph: 0740 69-5308.
Cooktown Motor Inn	Charlotte St. Ph: 0740 69-5357.
Hillcrest Holiday Lodge	Hope St. Ph: 0740 69-5305.
Milkwood Lodge	Annan Road. Ph: 0740 69-5007.
River of Gold Motel	Cnr Hope & Walker Sts. Ph: 0740 69-5222.
Seaview Motel	The Esplanade. Ph: 0740 69-5377.
Sovereign Resort	Charlotte St. Ph: 0740 69-5400.

Hostels

Cooktown Lodge & Backpackers	Charlotte St. Ph: 0740 69-5166.

Emergency Numbers

	Police:	0740 69-5320.
	Hospital:	0740 69-5433.

Department of Environment – Charlotte Street.

For information on Black Mountain, Mt. Cook, Endeavour River, Lakefield, Starcke & Cape Melville National Parks ph: 0740 69-5777. Fax: 0740 69-5574.

TRANSPORT FROM CAIRNS

Coach Services

Coral Coaches operate a daily service (except Monday) taking in both inland and coastal routes. Bookings are essential. For details contact:

Coral Coaches
Trinity Wharf
Wharf Street
Cairns Qld. 4870
Ph: 0740 31-7577 or 0740 98-2600 Fax: 0740 98-1064

Air Services

Flightwest currently service Cooktown daily. For details ph: Flightwest on 13 2392 anywhere in Queensland – 1800 777 879 elsewhere. Charter flights can be arranged through Wingz North. Ph: 0740 35-9032.

Cooktown to Musgrave via Lakefield National Park 295km

Travelling North from Cooktown, following the Endeavour River and out past the airport. At about the 35km point the road on your right leads off to Hopevale Mission. Straight ahead another 6km and you have to ford across the river at Isabella Falls. This is a great spot for a picnic and a rest. From Isabella the road winds up through the ranges, then drops down into the Normanby River Crossing. Before the crossing on your right is the turnoff to Melsonby Station where there is camping and accommodation. Ph/Fax: 0740 60-2259. Twenty metres upstream from the road crossing are some of the old pylons used in the construction of the old rail bridge that linked Cooktown and Laura around 1930. The track from the Normanby River to the Laura River, approximately 50km, passes along the Northern edge of the Battle Camp Ranges with their massive escarpments. This section of road passes through private pastoral holdings, so please leave gates as you find them and be very cautious of livestock.

The remains of the old rail bridge that crossed the Normanby River

There is strictly no camping along this section of track until you enter Lakefield National Park.

The Battle Camp Ranges were named after a group made up of approximately 130 diggers and police was attacked by around 500 massed Aboriginal war warriors, with many Aboriginal lives being lost in this confrontation.

Approximately 26km before the Laura River you enter the Lakefield National Park, so please obey all park rules. Early after the wet Laura River still can have quite a torrent of water flow, but dries up towards the end of the dry season.

Just over the river is the old abandoned Laura Homestead. Being vacated in the early 1960's, it is definitely worth a look. There is no camping permitted around the homestead.

0.5km past the old Laura Homestead there is a road entering from your right. Turn right here for the Ranger Station and the road to Musgrave. Turning left at this intersection takes you back to the Laura township. Turning right here and travelling up through Lakefield National Park with its well-signposted tracks and Ranger Stations.

Old Laura	– Deserted homestead, located between New Laura and Laura.
Laura	– Township – fuel, accommodation, limited facilities.
New Laura	– Ranger Station only, no fuels or supplies. Located in Lakefield National Park.
Lakefield Ranger Station	– No fuel or supplies. Located in Lakefield National Park.
Bizant Ranger Station	– No fuel or supplies. Located in Lakefield National Park.

Travelling North through Lakefield National Park, from the Old Laura Homestead to Musgrave, takes approximately five to six hours. For more detailed information see Lakefield National Park map, page 143 and Lakefield National Park information, page 141.

The deserted Homestead at Old Laura

Queensland Cape York Safari Operators

Billy Tea Safaris
P.O. Box 77N
Cairns North Qld. 4870
Ph: 0740 32-0077
Fax: 0740 32-0055

Australian Outback Safaris
42 Abbot Street
Cairns Qld. 4870
Ph: 0740 31-5833
Fax: 0740 31-5679

Australian Pacific Tours
107 Draper Street
Cairns Qld. 4870
Ph: 0740 51-9299
Fax: 0740 31-1075

Australian Wilderness Safari
P.O. Box 396
Mossman River Gorge
Ph: (0740) 98-1766
Fax: (0740) 98-1983

Cape York Connections
P.O. Box 371
Port Douglas Qld. 4871
Ph:/Fax: 0740 98-4938

Guides To Adventure
P.O. Box 908
Atherton Qld. 4883
Ph: 0740 91-1978
Fax: 0740 91-2545

Heritage 4WD tours
& Kamp Out Safaris
17 Penine Close
Smithfield Qld. 4876
Ph: 0740 38-2628
Fax: 0740 32-2186

Oz Safari Tours
P.O. Box 6464 CMC
Cairns Qld. 4870
Ph: 0740 55-9535
Fax: 0740 55-9918

Trezise Bush Guides
P.O. Box 106
Freshwater
Cairns Qld. 4870
Ph: 0740 55-1865
Fax: 0740 31-2016

Wilderness Challenge
P.O. Box 254
Cairns Qld. 4870
Ph: 0740 55-6504
Fax: 0740 57-7226

Wild Track Adventure Safaris
P.O. Box 2397
Cairns Qld. 4870
Ph: 0740 55-2247
Fax: 0740 58-1930

Tourist Information Centres

Far North Queensland Promotion Bureau
Cnr Grafton & Hartley Sts.
Cairns Qld. 4870
Ph: 0740 51-3588
Fax: 0740 51-0127

Queensland Tourist & Travel Corporation
Floor 36 Riverside Centre
123 Eagle Street Brisbane 4000
Ph: 07 3406 5400
Fax: 07 3406 5436

Queensland Government Travel Centre
196 Adelaide St.
Brisbane 4000
Ph: 131801
Fax: 07 3221 5320

Cooktown Tourism Association
P.O. Box 3
Cooktown Qld. 4871
Ph: 0740 69-5444

Cruise Ships to Cape York
Kangaroo Explorer
P.O. Box 7110
Cairns Mail Centre
Cairns Qld. 4870
Ph: Toll Free 1800 079 141
or 0740 32-4000

Air Services to Cape York

Ansett Airlines
Ph: 131300 (Australia Wide)

Flightwest Airlines
Ph: 132392

Sunstate Airlines
Ph: 131313 (Australia Wide)

Wingz North Aviation
Hangar 9
General Aviation Section
Cairns Airport
Ph: 0740 35-9032

Cape York Air Services
P.M.B. 13
Cairns Qld. 4871
Ph: 0740 35-9399
(Weekday service to Cape cattle
stations carrying mail & passengers)

Motorcycle Safaris

Motorcycle Adventure Safaris
Cape York Motorcycles Adventures
P.O. Box 105
Clifton Beach
Cairns Qld. 4870
Toll Free: 1800 643 743

Queensland National Parks and Wildlife Service

Dept. of Environment & Heritage
10-12 McLeod Street
Cairns Qld. 4870
Ph: 0740 52-3096
Fax: 0740 52-3080

4WD Hire

Hertz 4WD Rentals
436 Sheridan Street
Cairns Qld. 4870
Ph: 0740 53-6701

Marlin 4WD Rentals

440 Sheridan Street
Cairns Qld. 4870
Ph: 0740 32-3094

New Release

Lynn & Yvonne Fraser have released a second book in their travelling guide series titled "The Great Top Road". This publication explores the Gulf Savannah region which extends from Queensland through to the Northern Territory. They have extensively travelled the area detailing all information including travelling directions, maps, accommodation and camping and all points of interest with colour photographs capturing the area's beauty. This guide also includes travel for 2WD vehicles and the towing of caravans and campers. "The Great Top Road" is available from all bookshops and newsagencies throughout Australia at a cost of $24.95.